DOES CANADA MATTER?

DOES CANADA MATTER?

Liberalism and
the Illusion of Sovereignty

Joe,

Best Wishes,

Clarence Bolt

Dec 14/99

by

Clarence Bolt

RONSDALE PRESS
1999

DOES CANADA MATTER?
Copyright © 1999 Clarence Bolt

RONSDALE PRESS
3350 West 21st Avenue
Vancouver, B.C. Canada
V6S 1G7

Set in New Baskerville 11 on 16
Typesetting: Julie Cochrane, Vancouver, BC
Printing: Hignell Printing, Winnipeg, Manitoba
Cover Design: Julie Cochrane

Ronsdale Press wishes to thank the Canada Council for the Arts, the Government of Canada through the Book Publishing Industry Development Program (BPIDP), and the British Columbia Cultural Services Branch for their support of its publishing program.

CANADIAN CATALOGUING IN PUBLICATION DATA
Bolt, Clarence R.
   Does Canada matter?

   Includes bibliographical references and index.
   ISBN 0-921870-64-7

   1. Canada—Civilization—1945–   I. Title.
FC95.4.B64 1999   971.064'8   C98-911180-6
F1021.2.B64   1999

*Dedicated to
my grandfather, Jan Piers,
who understood in his everyday life
what George Grant attempted
to say philosophically.*

TABLE OF CONTENTS

PREFACE

It was the best of times, it was the worst
of times.
    — Charles Dickens, *A Tale of Two Cities*

1967: The Last Good Year
                — Pierre Berton (1997)

On the evening of October 30, 1995, Canadians sat glued to
their television sets in dismay as early results from the Quebec
referendum showed supporters for separation from Canada
winning by a narrow margin. By 10:00 p.m. (Eastern), the tide
had turned, and, by a margin of less than one percent, or
50,000 votes, the separatist option had been defeated.

It is not certain, however, how much longer Canadians committed to confederation will be able to keep Quebec in the country. Because previous provincial or regional secession movements
usually lacked momentum or widespread popular support,
Canadians have neglected to develop the skills, knowledge, or
experience to deal with threats to the integrity of Canada's territory.

In fact, as recently as fifty years ago, few Canadians (except,
perhaps, for academics or other such privileged few) thought

9

much about Canadian identity, separatism, or national sovereignty. Much more typical were people like my parents, post-World War II immigrants from Holland, who, along with hundreds of thousands of other young couples, whether newcomers like themselves or Canadian-born, saw Canada with its natural wealth, freedom, and opportunities as a safe and secure place to live, work, and raise families. From their perspective, it also did no harm that they lived next door to the United States of America, the "free" world's richest, most powerful country, its bulwark against Soviet communism. Canada's baby boom of the 1950s and early 1960s, the largest in the postwar west, reflected their optimism.

By and large, Canada delivered for them. My parents, for example, even while struggling to make ends meet, almost immediately bought a house and a car, and over the next twenty-five years paid for their children's private-school education, went on vacations, supported my grandparents, and so forth. They are now retired, pensioned and living off investments, in a mortgage-free house less than ten years old. They insist that they do not regret immigrating. They are happy with Canada.

I too am relatively happy with Canada. Born months after their arrival, I shared their hopes and aspirations, partaking in the country's rapid expansion of personal and collective wealth in the first three postwar decades, and benefitting from newly created, social-security programs. Few Canadians at the time considered that this expanding good life was reversible. That naiveté began to erode in the late-1970s as the country's major media began bombarding Canadians with accounts about growing government debt, social security programs that cost too much, unemployment, violence, environmental degradation, and domestic breakdown.

My parent's late-teenage and twenty-something grandchildren and their contemporaries, whom I regularly face in the classroom, who have been assaulted with these negative media messages all of their lives, are less upbeat about their future and far less sanguine about their country. Unlike their grandparents' generation which believed that the miseries of their youth (Depression, Nazism, and World War II) were detours on the road to a better future, they believe, despite relative affluence, that their materially comfortable present hides a future of diminishing possibilities. On January 24, 1998, *The Vancouver Sun* noted that "a recent survey of 1,000 Canadians under 30 turned up the startling statistic that 79 percent would seriously consider leaving Canada for better employment opportunities." Many of this age-group blame the lifestyles of their parents and grandparents as well as the policies of post-war governments for their bleak future. They exhibit a world-weariness and a lack of affection for their country which their parents and grandparents find surprising and disturbing in people so young, given the optimism they experienced at that age.

Nor does Canada's political scene offer them much comfort. The current dominant, so-called right-wing view, accepted by all federal, national parties in Canada, with the exception of the New Democratic Party (NDP), and represented by think-tanks such as the Fraser Institute, the C.D. Howe Institute, the Business Council on National Issues, and the Canadian Taxpayers' Federation, claims that the decline of living standards in the past two decades is the result of government debt (federal and provincial) and restrictions on Canadian corporations' ability to compete internationally. They blame punitive corporate taxes, excessive spending on social programs (which waste money and create lazy people), and undue regulation of labour and the environment for their problems. They demand that governments "create" a climate for a laissez-faire, market-driven economy, where private enterprise will run the world as much as possible. In a competitive, globalizing future, Canada will survive as a prosperous nation only if its business, corporate, and industrial sectors are free to compete without the crippling brakes of costly, interventionist, government policies and restrictive environmental and labour codes.

On the other side of the political spectrum, so-called left-leaning groups such as factions within the NDP, the Council of Canadians, the Canadian Centre for Policy Alternatives, and the Social Planning and Research Council argue that Canada's current social, economic, and political problems are, in fact, the result of federal and provincial governments' acceptance of precisely these views. Successive regimes under Brian Mulroney and Jean Chretien, they say, began "dismantling the nation" by deregulating business and industry, lowering taxes for the wealthy and corporations, permitting high interest rates which drove up federal debt, pursuing a fiscal policy which held inflation rather than unemployment as public enemy number one, and cutting social programs for the poor and needy. These policies produced high unemployment and widened the gap between the wealthy and the poor. Tony Clarke of the Canadian Centre for Policy Alternatives argues that right-wing ideologues are "reinvent[ing] the state as the political arm of big business." British Columbia's Finance Minister Andrew Petter noted on December 9, 1997: "Canadian unity comes from well-funded social programs." For both Clarke and Petter, a fair tax system, low interest rates, tough labour and environmental standards, and proper funding for social programs will help maintain a unified, sovereign Canada.

Most Canadians have problems with the extremes of both perspectives. Most agree with right-wing views that excessive debt is bad, that current tax rates are high, and that the country's social security network has problems. But most also acknowledge that unemployment (particularly for youth) and lack of job security threaten the country's social and economic order, that certain social programs (education and health, e.g.) are vital if Canada is to remain a just and fair society, and that environmental decline is a serious problem. They are dissatisfied with endless political rhetoric from both the right and the left; they trust and believe few politicians. Rather than participating in mainstream politics, if they have an interest in public affairs at all, increasing numbers are involved in issues which seem manageable and/or comprehensible. Hence, the rise of "interest" groups in fields such as education, crime, or the environment, or of "rights" movements in areas such as gender, ethnicity, or racial identity.

Unfortunately, this trend divides Canadians into ever smaller, antagonistic, narrowly-defined segments, characterized by what United States' political scientist Jean Bethke Elshtain, in her 1993 Massey Lectures, called the "politics of difference." Because they have never learned how, few Canadians seem to have the resolve, knowledge, or skill to address concepts such as the common good, national identity, or national sovereignty. Without these abilities, there is good reason to worry whether Canadians can engage in the necessary dialogue and take the appropriate steps to help Canada survive such threats to its future as Quebec separatism.

Canadians should not delude themselves into thinking that the close October 30, 1995 result removed this threat. It merely strengthened the resolve of Quebec separatists. Within three months, their inspirational leader, Lucien Bouchard, became the premier of Quebec, promising a series of referenda until he gets the outcome that he wants. The innocuous Calgary Declaration of October 1997 illustrates the inability of current federal and provincial leaders to produce meaningful alternatives to separatism or to inspire Canadians to rally around their country. The choice of Jean Charest as leader of the Liberal Party in late April 1998 recharged the federalist forces in Quebec, and although the Parti Quebecois won the majority of seats in a provincial election on November 30, 1998, the Liberals obtained larger popular support, by a narrow margin of approximately 43% to 42%. However successful Charest may ultimately be, he and other federalists are not likely to undermine the determination of separatists.

But the problem of Canada's future is not confined to Quebec. Outside of Quebec, more and more Canadians are willing to accept the loss of that province. In the 1993 and 1997 federal elections, the Reform Party, led by Preston Manning and campaigning on an anti-Quebec platform, swept the majority of ridings west of Manitoba; east of Manitoba, however, except for one seat in Ontario in 1993, they were shut out. Ironically, since 1993, the Reform and the separatist Bloc Quebecois parties, neither of which believes in historic Canada, have been Canada's largest opposition parties.

A significant number of western Canadians are willing to go even further and entertain the idea of western Canadian separatism. A poll conducted by POLLARA between November 28 and December 2, 1997, for example, indicated that 50 percent of British Columbians claimed to be unhappy with their province's lot in Confederation, 25 percent believing that British Columbia would be better off outside Canada.[1]

But current political realities, whether the right/left split or the threat of the dismemberment of Canada, tell only part of the story. The reason behind the fear about the loss of Quebecois culture in an Anglophone Canada, which has been responsible for spurring many Quebec nationalists to their separatist views, ought also to be the concern of Canadians worried about the fate of a distinct and sovereign Canada, not just in North America but in the emerging global world. In the next century, the central question, not only in Canada but around the world will be whether unique cultures and nations will be able to survive current globalizing trends in economics, production, and mass entertainment (especially TV), or if humanity's linguistic, religious, political, economic, and social variety will be reduced to little more than choices about surface values such as sportswear (Nike versus Reebok), sexual orientation, television shows, "ethnic" dishes, or soccer teams.

The following chapters will define the issues at stake in maintaining a sovereign Canada. The first chapter sets the context by examining the current state of the country and the issues that confront Canadians as the ideology of globalization takes ever deeper root in the policies and actions of the country's media, corporate, and political elites, while at the same time everyday Canadians grow increasingly cynical about their leaders' ability to keep the country together or to serve the common good. At the heart of Canada's current crisis is its elite's acceptance of a liberal ideology which has dominated western countries since the late eighteenth century.

Subsequent chapters will examine how this liberal ideology has shaped Canada since 1867, particularly its economic structures; how it has fostered a competitive regionalism which has made it difficult for various regions of the country to share a unified vision and identity; how it has created the everyday "structures" in which most Canadians live, sleep, work, and play; and, finally, how it has penetrated the country's collective and personal space by means of the myths which underpin it.

The book will then examine the heart of the issue, namely, the premises of liberal ideology. It will argue that liberalism's impact has been devastating not only for the survival of Canadian sovereignty but for the well-being of all unique national, cultural, linguistic, regional, and community identities. It will offer suggestions for restoring the health of the communities and regions in which Canadians live so that they can feel that they belong to their communities and to their regions, that is, that they can be content with the places they call *home*. While some observers of the Canadian scene believe that strong regions stand in the way of a unified and healthy country, Canada will function and remain sovereign only if its regions and communities are unique, strong, and healthy. A country is as weak as its weakest parts. The whole will not function if the parts do not "work." The book will conclude by arguing that Canada can remain sovereign only if its citizens begin to challenge the liberal assumptions which have shaped the country since confederation.

The crucial — and unanswered — question is whether Canadians can resist the blandishments of the liberal dream and take the steps necessary to preserve Canada's sovereignty.

NOTES

1 The same poll had 50 percent of Quebecers feeling dissatisfied with Canada, and 31 percent believing they would be better off outside Canada.

1

THE SETTING

"In xenetia — in exile," said Athos . . . "in a foreign landscape, a man discovers the old songs. He calls out for water from his own well, for apples from his own orchard, for the muscat grapes from his own vine."

"What is man," said Athos, "who has no landscape? Nothing but mirrors and tides."

— Anne Michaels, *Fugitive Pieces*

In his 1965 *Lament for a Nation: The Defeat of Canadian Nationalism,* philosopher George Grant mourned the passing of Canada: "To lament is to cry out at the death or at the dying of something loved. Lamentation is not an indulgence in despair or cynicism. In a lament for a child's death, there is not only pain and regret, but also celebration of passed good." He lamented that Canada was losing its "soul" to what he called the "homogenizing" forces of modernity as embodied in the liberal, American, capitalist empire.

Those who cared about Canada were deeply moved and

saddened by his lament. But few Canadians felt inspired by Grant's warning to take quick action to save the country from continentalization by the Americans. At the root of the problem, he argued, was the shared commitment by Canadians and Americans to modern technology with its homogenizing tendencies. Canada's elites and its general population, if they were even paying attention, smiled and nodded politely, dismissing Grant's despair as the rantings of a cranky, conservative philosopher. No one, at the time, considered the possibility that within half a decade of his writing, the forces of Quebec separatism would render Canada's borders insecure. Canadians and their leaders were, as John Ralston Saul puts it, an "unconscious society," paying little attention to the development of the forces which have been, and still are, undoing their country. The validity of Grant's perception about Canada's future was made clear in Francis Fukuyama's recent proposition that the end of the cold war has finished "mankind's ideological evolution," and that we are now witnessing the "universalization of western *liberal* [emphasis mine] democracy as the final form of human government."

Grant was particularly distressed that Canada's elites, particularly Liberal governments from Mackenzie King to Lester Pearson, and their allies in the media and corporate worlds, were encouraging, even welcoming, these trends. He mourned the end of nineteenth-century conservatism with its emphasis on community and its respect for tradition. He was critical of John Diefenbaker, whom he saw as the last hope for an independent Canada, but who, he believed, had squandered the opportunity to preserve Canada's sovereignty because he was incapable of standing up to the concentrated attacks on him and his views by North America's liberal "ruling classes."

18

Following the defeat of the Diefenbaker Conservatives in 1963, the Pearson and Trudeau Liberal Governments of the 1960s, 1970s and early 1980s did make some attempts to develop and enhance Canadian identity, a need identified by several Royal Commissions, starting with the Massey Commission (1949-1951). Social programs such as Medicare and pensions, a home-grown Canadian flag, multiculturalism, the Federal Investment Review Agency, the National Energy Policy, restrictions on foreign content in the media, the CRTC, and other such measures were designed to build a North American society distinct from that of the United States. But these measures barely masked the integration of Canada with the United States, as shown by Canadians' uncritical acceptance of United States' popular culture — whether it be movies, music, pulp literature, mass magazines, television, or professional sports — and a commitment to a way of life based on economic growth, technological development, suburban sprawl, and automobile mobility. In short, Canada was increasingly being defined by what Grant described as United States' style "liberalism."

Grant's brief flicker of hope when the Liberal Party he so disliked was defeated in 1984 by Brian Mulroney's Progressive Conservative Party died as he and like-minded citizens of Canada watched with dismay as a party bearing the name Conservative attacked what many people had come to see as central to a developing Canadian identity: the CBC, the national railway system, the social security network, the national energy program, the Federal Investment Review Agency, and various other crown corporations. Many of these initiatives had been designed to defy Canada's geography and unify its diverse regions. The 1989 Free Trade Agreement with the United States completed this attack by officially opening up the borders between the two countries, integrating their economies, and removing the last vestiges of protection for Canada's indigenous business sector.[1]

The return to power of the Liberal Party in 1993 and its commitment to the economic and trade policies of the Mulroney Conservatives has ensured that hopes for the recovery of Canada's sovereignty are quixotic at best. The record of the Jean Chretien-led Liberal Party is as bad as, if not worse than, that of the Tories. Despite their earlier objection to the Free Trade Agreement, the Liberals kept it in place. In fact, they took the Progressive Conservative approach to foreign trade a step further subsequently by signing the North American Free Trade Agreement (NAFTA) with the United States and Mexico, and a free trade deal with Chile (no doubt because of its sterling human rights record since Allende). During the 1997 election campaign it was revealed that the Liberals were negotiating with 28 other countries to create a Multilateral Agreement on Investment (MAI), allegedly a corporate charter of rights in which clauses in the agreement protecting the rights and privileges of trans-national corporations would supersede local, state/provincial, and national laws and powers of the national signatories. In April of 1998, Canada's Jean Chretien led an attempt to create a hemispheric free trade zone, including most of the countries of the Americas. The United States did not participate in the discussions because of Cuba's inclusion in the talks.

The Liberals have thus not only maintained the Progressive Conservatives' trade and tariff policies but also their domestic approach. In the name of fiscal restraint, they have continued dismantling equalization policies and social programs, privatizing crown corporations, devolving areas of federal responsibility to the provinces, and cutting funds to institutions such as the CBC. Surprisingly, this undoing of Canada's historic mechanisms of governance, and this un-making of its traditional institutions, is happening with little fanfare, as if what the Liberals are doing is natural, inevitable. Many Canadians are naively applauding these efforts, while even more offer only token opposition to initiatives such as taxpayer-funded, government-sponsored (and led), trade missions of Canada's political, media, business, and corporate leaders to Asia and Latin America. Few blinked when Chretien nicknamed these missions "Team Canada," as if profit-motivated forays by Canada's elites to make "deals" with countries with appalling human rights records is little more than sport, similar to a Canada/Russia hockey series.

At the same time that he was lamenting Canada's loss of sovereignty, Grant noted that the country's political scene offered no viable options to liberalism. This has not changed. Like Canada's two original national parties, the third one, the New Democratic Party (a watered down version of the Cooperative Commonwealth Federation, the only real alternative to mainstream parties that Canada ever had), and the two new ones, the Reform Party of Canada and the separatist Bloc Quebecois, all embrace what Grant defined as the liberal point of view.

By liberal, he did not mean the everyday definition of "liberal," that is, "free from prejudice and bigotry; tolerant; open-minded; generous; willing to give in large amounts; not strict, etc." Nor did he use the word as many in the political arena currently do, associating it with modern, reformist, government-interventionist, political practice, in contrast to "conservative" or "neo-conservative" practice, that is, traditional, laissez-faire, free-enterprise politics.

Instead, he meant a political philosophy that had emerged in Europe by the late eighteenth-century, one which, as we approach the twenty-first century, has become the only option in western countries such as Canada. Just as Catholics and Protestants share similar fundamental Christian beliefs, so too do today's "liberals" and "neo-conservatives" share a base of political ideas and practices derived from a common, liberal source, the product of the breakdown of the late medieval, early-modern, Christian, divine-right concept of monarchical rule held by most European kings, queens, and princes of the time.

After the savage, religious wars between Protestant and Catholic monarchs in the sixteenth and seventeenth centuries, some of the leading minds of the day concluded that a better foundation and sounder principles for government could be derived from the "new science" of astronomers, scientists, and mathematicians such as Copernicus, Galileo, Kepler, and Bacon. These "new sciences" purported, on the basis of the observation of nature and through the use of reason, to have discovered unequivocally *true* laws governing natural phenomena such as planetary relationships and motion. Why not, some of the brightest minds of the day argued, attempt a broader application of these methods? Would not societies and systems of government based on the laws of nature and "instrumental" reason rather than on superstition and "irrational" impulses have the potential to end religious strife and to lift humanity to unprecedented peace, unlimited wealth, and perpetual happiness?

And so was born the Enlightenment, lasting roughly from 1650 to 1800. It proceeded from the premise that the universe (nature) was rational, orderly and machine-like (mechanistic), and that all of its mysteries could be uncovered if the correct questions were asked of it and appropriate, empirical method(s) were used to determine the answers. The Enlightenment created a distinction between "objective" truth (derived from nature and measurable, quantifiable, and provable — i.e., reliable) and "subjective" speculation (the product of imagination and opinion, i.e., unreliable).

By the eighteenth century, these principles, applied to politics and legal theory, had created what has been called liberalism. One of its most famous proponents was the late seventeenth-century English philosopher, John Locke, who rejected the medieval view of society as an organic entity and of government and monarchical authority as having divine origin. Instead, he looked to nature, and concluded that society was a collection of individuals. He located the basis for governmental authority in the governed, namely, the people, whom he defined as equal *individuals* with inherent *natural rights* to life, liberty, and property.

Liberals such as Locke saw government's primary purpose as being to protect each individual's freedom to exercise his/her fundamental, natural rights and liberties. Governments should not be involved with religion or metaphysics, nor should they concern themselves with business and commerce which should be free to follow the natural laws of economics (laissez-faire or free enterprise). In short, the purpose of governments was to ensure an environment in which neither they nor other institutions would stand in the way of individual freedom. Given the dominance of aristocratic, ecclesiastical, and monarchical elements at the time, of the brutal conflicts which they had engendered since the late Medieval period, and of their rather callous disregard for the lives of ordinary people, liberal concepts seemed sensible, even liberating. Charles Taylor has argued that the liberal ideal of "authenticity," which includes the ideas that "each of us has an original way of being human" and that each individual can both recognize and realize his/her "own fulfilment," is an invaluable insight of liberalism. And so it is! However, in a fashion similar to that of late eighteenth- and early nineteenth-century political conservatives such as Edmund Burke and Joseph Marie de Maistre, he has grave concerns about the danger of dealing that card alone, particularly about the liberal denigration of history, tradition, and (fixed) eternal values, and its elevation of individual rights over the worth of the civic community.

By 1900, the victory of liberalism over political conservatism in western political practice had been assured. Nonetheless, the word "conservative" has remained in the political lexicon. Today's "neo-conservatism," as practised by Preston Manning or Newt Gingrich, despite its vilification of "liberal" politics, is not, strictly speaking, conservatism in the traditional sense of the word. In reality, it is a variant of original liberalism, more akin to the views of those who currently wear the label "liberal" than those of traditional conservatives.

The similarity stems from the fact that today's "liberals" and "neo-conservatives" both subscribe to similar ideals of individual rights and elective government. Both accept the eighteenth-century concept of the rapid growth of productive forces through industrial/commercial expansion and technological innovation to satisfy individual desires, and both identify the ability to meet individual needs as progress (see chapter 6). They differ only in their opinion about the role that governments should play in achieving this end, with "liberals" arguing for significant government involvement in areas such as economics, education, welfare, and labour, but a minor role in ethics and morality. Conversely, "neo-conservatives" argue for laissez-faire economics but for state intervention in ethical matters and personal morality, advocating what many of them euphemistically call "family values" (ironically, neo-conservatism's individualistic, economic values contradict its "ethics"). The differences between the two are ones of emphasis, not of philosophy — hence the conclusion, similar to that of Grant's in the 1960s, that in countries like Canada, there presently are no significant alternatives to liberalism. For that reason, it is more accurate to label today's "neo-conservatives" as "neo-liberals," the word that will be used for them from this point.

But liberalism does not exist in a vacuum. As Grant noted in 1965, Canadians ought also to be aware of a number of other Enlightenment ideals which accompany liberalism because these too are accepted without question by Canada's five major political parties as well as by most citizens.

The first of these ideals — liberal democracy — rose from the liberal assumption of the natural rights of each individual. John Locke argued that because government authority came from the "consent of the governed," the policies and legislation of governments should be divined from the wishes of the electorate, the "collective reason" of the citizenry.

Initially, liberal democracy, as practised in Europe and North America, defined the "rational electorate" narrowly, allowing suffrage and participation to a limited number of people, usually only those with religious, property, or status qualifications. Gradually, however, the enshrining of individual rights in constitutions and/or legislation forced liberal democratic governments to embrace universal suffrage. It made little sense to argue for universal individual rights and the "consent of the governed" while at the same time excluding significant numbers of adult citizens from the electoral process.

But liberal democracy is not democracy in the true sense of the word, which literally means power, government, and authority in the hands of the people. The expansion of suffrage in the eighteenth and nineteenth centuries did not change the power structures or the authority of the elites. In 1831, for example, Thomas Babington Macaulay supported giving the vote to the British middle class because it would be far less "violent" or "calamitous" than having them revolt. It would be "a measure of reform: but I support it still more as a measure of conservation. We must admit those whom it may be safe to admit." It was best, he concluded, to give them a "place in the system."

William Gladstone said much the same in 1866 when Britain's Parliament was considering giving the working classes the vote. He noted that the working classes had been improving themselves steadily, citing rising levels of literacy and savings: "I say distinctly that we are not going to hand over the power to the [working classes] at all. There is no proof whatever that the working classes if enfranchised, would act together as a class." The same points about threats to the status quo were raised in early twentieth-century debates about female suffrage in countries such as Canada.

In practice, rather than democracy, Canada has a party system of government, in which, once every two to five years, adult citizens have the right to elect a party to govern them. As two Polish graduate students, Jacek Kuron and Karol Modzelewski, argued in 1965 about Parliamentary democracies when they were calling for the reform of the Polish communist government, "Even in the most perfect forms, they are not governments of the people. . . . the parties fight only to be elected.

The moment the vote is cast, the electoral plan is thrown in the wastebasket." Elected officials are bound only to the party which named them as candidates. Citizens, they concluded, are organized into arbitrary electoral districts, and their participation in politics amounts

> ... to nothing more than reading statements of leaders in the press, listening to them on the radio, and seeing them on TV — and once every 4 or 5 years voting to choose the party to govern them. The rest takes place by virtue of a mandate, without the voters' participation. Furthermore, parliaments only exercise legislative power. The executive apparatus holds the only real power.

The Procurator of the Holy Synod of the Russian Orthodox Church from 1880-1905, Konstantin Pobedonostsev called parliamentary democracy "the great falsehood of our time":

> [In] theory . . . , the rational majority must rule; in practice, the party is ruled by five or six of its leaders who exercise all power. In theory, decisions are controlled by clear arguments in . . . Parliamentary debates; in practice, they . . . are determined by the wills of the leaders and the promptings of personal interest. In theory, the representatives of the people consider only the public welfare; in practice, their first consideration is their own advancement, and the interests of their friends. In theory, the elector gives his vote for his candidate because he knows and trusts him; in practice, the elector gives his vote for a man whom he seldom knows, but who has been forced on him by the speeches of an interested party.

He had a point. The concept of the natural rights of each individual, enshrined in constitutions throughout the western world, has yet to find its place in actual government practice in most liberal democracies which, despite rhetoric to the contrary, still exist largely to promote the interests of elites rather than those of the broader electorate. Indeed, one of the more significant obstacles to fuller democracy in Canada may be the myth that Canadians already have it.

A second product of the Enlightenment, industrialization, which emerged in the late eighteenth and early nineteenth centuries, was simply the application of the Enlightenment's rational, machine-like view of the universe to work. If nature was mechanistic, objective, and neutral, one could easily rationalize harnessing its power by using its own laws to produce advanced machines (technology) which would be "perfections" of nature. Nature, in contrast to beliefs of cultures all over the world, would be treated as "object," without value in its own right. Industrialization and modern technology (see chapter 5) became perfect marriage partners.

Wherever industrialization occurred, the nature of work was altered, subsistence living being replaced by cash labour. As Marx and Engels noted in 1848, the specialized, skilled labour of artisans and craftsmen was made redundant by "new methods of production," namely, by factories, which were oriented to unskilled labour and mass-production. Not only were workers "placed under the command of a perfect hierarchy of officers and sergeants" (a military model) but "they are daily and hourly enslaved by the machine, by the over-looker, and, above all, by the individual bourgeois manufacturer himself." The ever greater reliance on regimented labour and on the productive capacity of machines has continued unabated since. Industrialization has challenged the ability of local communities and regions to be self-sustaining because it has tied work and production to ever larger corporate structures, the most powerful of which now straddle the globe.² Correspondingly, nature's wealth, whether fish, forests, or minerals, is being plundered at ever faster rates.

A third product, capitalism, with roots in late medieval market-systems, was the twin of industrialization. The Enlightenment criteria of nature and reason were applied to exchange, which, it was argued, should be free to follow *natural* laws of supply and demand. Traditional ideas about wealth as the ownership of tangibles which distinguished the possessor from those who lacked such possessions was replaced by a more fluid notion of wealth, namely, that of the acquisition and accumulation of capital. Through investment, capital would generate profit, by which was meant ever larger amounts of capital. Goods *and* services became commodities, their intrinsic worth replaced by cash-value, that is, capital-worth.

The impact of capitalism has been dramatic. Prior to the modern era, the economic aspect of most people's lives was merely one function among many. Capitalism's reduction of goods and services to commodities has elevated the importance of the economic part of peoples' lives, making it the defining context in which most of life's other functions now occur. The "market" has been altered from a locale, a square, a specific place where people met and traded, to the space that delimits most of their activities. The merchant has become an entrepreneur, land a commodity to be bought and sold, usury legal, people consumers, and consumption the measure of life's value. Capitalism, economist Robert Heilbroner argues, thinks only in terms of "saleable goods."³

Heilbroner gives the market-system much credit for creating the context which made the modern, industrial/technological revolution possible, from the water-powered factories of the eighteenth century to today's electronic production systems. And, wherever the new socio-economic environments in the western world have been successfully created, material conditions have improved markedly. But, he adds, there have been costs. For one thing, new class relationships have divided those who own the means of production from those who labour. More importantly, there has been a serious drain of wealth from underdeveloped peripheries to the developed centres. From the agricultural enclosure movements to the factory systems of the eighteenth and nineteenth centuries to today's third-world sweat-shops, misery has been inherent in the modern capitalist economic order, a precondition for its success. The "market-economy," Heilbroner concludes, is the "attentive servant of the rich and deaf bystander of the poor."

In their 1848 *Communist Manifesto,* Karl Marx and Friedrich Engels noted that "the conditions of bourgeois society are too narrow to comprise the wealth created by them." Capitalists, they argued, are a beleaguered species, always feeling pressure from competitors threatening to enter their markets and steal their profits. To survive, they cut their costs by mechanizing (cutting workers), pushing the remaining workers harder, and launching new products. Marx and Engels predicted that not even globalization of markets could prevent capitalism from reaching the limits of expansion and from being destroyed by overproduction.

To this point, the destruction of capitalism has been avoided because of the intermediary role of the state. But Marx and Engels were not far off when they noted that modern states were simply the handmaidens of capitalist expansion, protecting and promoting the interests of capitalist classes at the expense of the common people: "The executive of the modern

State is but a committee for managing the common affairs of the bourgeoisie." In our day, the "laws of the market place" as promoted by capitalism have been uncritically accepted by most of Canada's government leaders and elites as objective "laws" which must be "obeyed." Ultimately, however, time will likely prove correct Marx and Engels' notion that there are limits to expansion.

It is important to note that the changes of the last two hundred years engendered by liberalism and corresponding Enlightenment ideals have not been all bad. Liberal democracy's emphasis on individual rights has freed many people to recognize their self-worth and to cherish individual difference and uniqueness. Technology and industrialization have been instrumental in extending life-expectancy in the western world and in improving the quality of life for many people. Capitalism has opened the doors for remarkable systems of distribution for goods and services.

But two hundred years is a very short time by which to evaluate the ultimate worth of Enlightenment ideals. On his death bed, more than twenty years ago, when asked what he thought about the French Revolution (1789), Chinese communist leader Chou En Lai reportedly said that it was too soon to say. In a Chinese proverb, one rock comments to another, as they stare out over a grove of ancient trees, "Life is transitory — trees come and trees go." While it may also be premature to assess definitively the impact of the liberal ideal of treating the natural environment as an object to be manipulated for industrial growth and capitalist development, there is growing evidence to support the thesis that much of its impact has not been positive for nature, whether measured in terms of the growing extinction of plant and animal species or the declining quality

of air, soil, and water. In short, while more time may be necessary for a definitive post-mortem on the Enlightenment, there
is growing evidence of long-term negative effects upon those
very elements necessary to sustain human and other life.

What is clear, however, is that, even since Grant's lament,
liberalism and the Enlightenment package of ideals have taken
an ever firmer hold of Canada and are continuing to challenge
its sovereignty. Jean Chretien's approach to governance is precisely the kind of politics about which Grant complained, and
the powerful elites whom he blamed for selling out Canada in
the 1950s and 1960s are still controlling the country's dominant institutions. To Grant's fears about the motivations of
Canada's elites must now be added concern about the influence and goals of international elites. As Linda McQuaig, in
Shooting the Hippo: Death by Deficit and other Canadian Myths
(1995), has persuasively argued, Canada's elites are increasingly taking their marching orders from global entities such as the
International Monetary Fund (IMF) and the World Bank, a
handful of international currency speculators, and foreign
bond-rating agencies. A select group of corporations and char-
tered banks are making record profits while everyday people
and small businesses are being buried ever more deeply under
mountains of debt because their costs are increasing faster
than their income. Most Canadians are quiescent because they
have accepted the argument, promoted by the corporate sector
and right-wing think tanks, that Canada's federal government's
symbiotic relationship with the corporate sector is for the economic well-being and long-term health of both the country and
its people.

Indeed, around the globe, governments are adopting similar political/economic practices, threatening, as Grant argued

in 1965, not only Canadian identity, but unique cultures, languages, and identities everywhere. Governments, and the elites that prop them up, are accepting, even encouraging, the spread of global, trans-national corporations, whose loyalties are to profit margins rather than to workers or to nature. Tom Frank has argued that "Corporations have become the dominant institutions of our time, occupying the position of the church in the Middle Ages and the nation-state of the past two centuries." In *Silent Coup*, Tony Clarke points out that, in early 1997, two hundred of these giant corporations controlled a quarter of the world's economic activity, with $7.1 trillion dollars of revenue as compared to $3.9 trillion for eighty percent of the world's population, yet they employ less than "a third of one one hundredth of one percent of the world's people." Of the world's 100 largest economies, 51 were corporations and 49 were countries. Wal-Mart's economic power was greater than that of 161 of the world's approximately two hundred countries. The United Nations' "Human Development Report, 1996," noted that 358 billionaires have wealth equalling that of the poorest 45 percent of the world's population.

But the rich are experiencing problems with that wealth. In their rush for profits, trans-national corporations, driven by an international economic elite, have devised ever cheaper and more efficient means to produce goods. One of these has been the displacement of workers in the industrialized world by low-wage ghettos in so-called third world countries. The workers in these low-wage workforces are seldom paid enough to buy the products that they are producing. There is a second group of casualties of this displacement, namely, the growing number of people in the industrialized world who are experiencing diminishing purchasing power because jobs are being moved out of their countries to these low wage areas, resulting in higher levels of unemployment and less disposable income. Consequently, there are increasing amounts of goods available without buyers. In short, as Marx and Engels predicted, the capital accumulation of the wealthy is beginning to exceed levels of consumption; there is only so much that can be bought.

This excess capital, instead of being spent on actual goods and services produced and used by people, now swirls through financial houses and banks around the globe, where so-called financial experts gamble with it with virtually no checks on their behaviour — on commodities, currencies, bonds, stocks, mutual funds, and a myriad of other instruments created only for speculation (a rich person's version of lottery tickets and bingo parlours). As Tony Clarke notes, "Speculative investment . . . has replaced productive investment." He points out that in 1997 $2 trillion (United States) circulates daily — with telecommunications systems capable of expanding that amount to $13 trillion (United States) — an amount that exceeds daily international trade in goods and services by sixty times. Decades ago, John Maynard Keynes warned governments that they needed to tighten investment controls and trade regulations when the amount of capital circulating had reached twice the level of trade.

In such an environment and in the face of such power, people have little direct control over their everyday lives, that is, over their labour, over the natural environment upon which they rely, or over the local communities in which they live. They have become ever more dependent upon homogeneous, industrial, mass-produced goods, non-renewable fossil fuels, massive energy projects, or agribusiness-produced foods. As a result, everyday life everywhere is becoming blandly identical —

witness the global reach of products such as Coca-Cola, Big Macs, or "Baywatch." Independent cultures and states cannot hope to survive if such trends continue unabated. Nor can Canada be a distinct and sovereign state.

This is particularly true because, rather than fighting for sovereignty, Canada's governments and elites are complying with and accepting the forces of globalization and homogenization, believing that the move to create a global market-place, directed by private, profit-oriented, trans-national, corporate structures, is the natural, inevitable direction for humanity's march to the future over which they have little power or control. By accepting this doctrine and by loosening controls and regulations on trans-national corporations, they are, in essence, abdicating their responsibility to ensure the common good and handing it over to non-elected entities that have no long-term commitment to the best interests of the "customers" they are serving.[3]

We have gone far beyond the rhetoric of leaders such as former United States' President Ronald Reagan and British Prime Minister Margaret Thatcher who believed that the role of government was merely to create the environment and set the stage for a flourishing, self-regulating, free-enterprise economy. By August, 1998, the United States and other leading industrial economies had poured well over $100 billion (United States) not only into the so-called "tiger economies" of Korea, Thailand, and Indonesia, but also into those of two of the world's most powerful countries, Japan and Russia, in order to prevent the collapse of the international market and financial system. Thus, instead of creating a self-regulating market-place (which supposedly can correct itself), the elites who are heading today's most powerful governments are taking no chances

on seeing the breakdown of the trans-national, corporate system, and are using their powers and the funds available to them
to assist this system in its effort to rebuild the world according
to their corporate vision. As Maude Barlow notes, "Governments everywhere, including ours in Canada, are in full retreat
before this corporate juggernaut, abandoning their citizens
(they call it empowering) to deal with corporations directly.
[C]orporate rule has replaced government rule." Globalization
is about trans-national corporations and banks having as few
restriction as possible in order to make ever larger profits, paying as little in taxes as possible, and even allowing governments
to go bankrupt if they do not cut services for ordinary people to
the bone.

For Canadians, this abdication of governmental responsibility makes much more difficult the attempt, since 1867, to
forge a unique, sovereign Canada and to generate genuine
feelings of commonality among people living in a far-flung geographical area with diverse regions, traditions, histories, and
everyday experience.

This task was never simple. R. Cole Harris has noted that
right from the earliest days of European settlement, neither the
French nor the English had a "master plan, . . . [a] vision, as in
New England, of Old World regeneration overseas." The popu-
lating of Canada by non-Natives was sporadic. Each European
settlement resembled an "island of light" in an archipelago,
separated (and connected) by snow, ice, muskeg, prairies, and
mountains:

> There was no continuous, expansive Canadian experience
> with the land. What was common was the lack of continuity
> imparted by the close limits of confined lands. Settlement
> proceeded in patches, island by island. One island would fill

up, then people would emigrate. Different islands were settled at different times with different technologies and economies by people from different backgrounds.

As a result, most citizens' concept of Canada and of Canadian
identity came to be defined by, and also largely confined to,
their experience of the islands which they inhabited. Harris
notes that it was in the "immediate horizon" of everyday experience, "the rhythms of the land, the traditional ways that earned
a living, and the people who lived nearby" that people defined
their identity. This has been true for people in settlements
across the country.

Nonetheless, a Canadian identity and feeling, a sense of
commonality, did develop, Harris argues, because of modern
communications networks, such as national railroads, radio
(especially the CBC), airlines, highways, and television. Pierre
Berton has pointed out how the railways, for example, gave
people and communities all across the country an imaginative
sense of being part of something bigger, as trains pulled into
and out of their towns to and from other parts of the country.
After World War II, federal government systems such as equalization payments and social security networks further cemented
ties among Canadians across the country. As Harris points out,
however, for many Canadians, their sense of Canada has simply
"grown out of the continuing experience of being here," and
attachments are primarily to their "islands."

Yet, as noted earlier, more Canadians are feeling less happy
about the places that they call home, increasingly complaining
about high taxes, crime, sewage disposal problems, garbage
buildup, destruction of natural bio-diversity, loss of local business and industry, or the diminution of community feeling.
Their choices for politicians often reflect protest rather than

affirmations of politicians or their political parties. This loss of good feeling has important repercussions, especially for a country such as Canada. When the "islands" with which Canadians identify themselves as Canadians lose their sense of cohesion and their feeling of common purpose with other regions, the country's fragile sense of unity is at risk.

And it is liberalism and its Enlightenment partners, trumpeting the virtues of globalization, which are a major factor in creating this uneasiness among Canadians, and which, therefore, are threatening fragile feelings of unity. At first glance, such attribution may appear to be far-fetched. But because ideals and value-systems are often unnoticed assumptions playing a key role in shaping the practises of everyday life, Canadians often do not fully see or understand the implications of liberalism and its Enlightenment partners. There is little doubt that their latest products, globalization and modern technology, are destroying local diversity in favour of homogeneity, and taking away *local* control over how people work, feed, move, amuse, clothe, or house themselves by placing this control in the hands of large, anonymous, corporate structures with few ties to where people actually live. As a result, people are feeling increasingly disconnected from each other and uprooted from the land. Historian Arthur Lower has noted that "the soul of Canada [must come] from the land," that is, from the place where its people live their daily lives, the implication being that Canada will lose its soul if its people feel disconnected from the places where they live.

American writer, Charlene Spretnak, argues that a sense of belonging, a feeling of place, is essential to human health. She points out that a major obstacle to the spread of the global, liberal way of life is a strong sense of attachment to "a place."

Trans-national corporations succeed in their drive for profit and dominance only after they have eliminated the power and resistance of peoples' sense of home, their local attachments, and replaced them with the ideals and products of a homogenous, modern world.

The success of trans-national corporatism is a major reason why many Canadians, particularly those from anonymous, homogeneous, suburban developments, are discontented. They see little that distinguishes their communities, their jobs, their environments, or their lives from those of suburbanites anywhere else in North America. They have little sense of "home" as they move restlessly from one part of the continent to another. Trevor Turner notes that human beings experience a natural discomfort at being in the "wrong place": "What [goes] on day by day around you in terms of people, smells, what you [see] and what you absorb, [keeps] your mind in balance." He points out that the word "nostalgia," first coined in 1688, comes from two Greek words, *nostos* (return home) and *algos* (pain); it described a longing that one felt when away from home. Current modern urban and suburban environments, he adds, "while safe, comfortable, and much longed for by occupants of inner cities or slums, may not provide a sense of home. Home is about difference."

For many Canadians, the rootlessness goes deeper. As Canadian writer Nancy Huston notes about her experience of Alberta:

> We [Europeans] were not even "returning," as the Israelis did, to a land we believed to be holy land. We calmly and firmly appropriated the holy lands of the Indians, despite all their resistance and protest. We were stronger than they were; it was as simple as that. And we did not, perhaps could

not, sacralize these lands in turn. That's the way it is — the New World is a desacralized world. . . .

In Quebec, there has not been a great deal more bloodshed than in Alberta, but a great deal more time has gone by. The Quebecois have reaped the benefits of what we Albertans lack so cruelly: namely, centuries in which to elaborate traditions, transmit memories, tell and retell the stories of our ancestors. The problem is that our own past will never acquire this sacred quality, because we Albertans were born and raised in the age of the radio and the telephone, the airplane and the moving picture, the television and the computer. Never again, at least in the Western World, will societies have the chance to evolve in relative isolation from one another. Distances have been reduced to nothing, with the result that the four pillars of culture — food, music, religion, and language — are standardized, instantaneous, homogenized.

Most Canadians have tenuous roots in this country, and for that reason the erosion of what little sense of place they experience carries a high price. To put it simply, if Canada's "islanders" lose this sense of place, Canada's identity, as well as its sovereignty, is at risk.

This is not to imply that every aspect of globalization is destructive of local communities and cultures. In the last three or four decades, for example, global communications technologies have allowed ever larger numbers of people to experience the interconnectedness of events and trends around the globe. They have made increasing numbers of people aware of issues such as the overuse of fossil fuels, rainforest destruction, the automobile culture, chemical production, agribusiness, the green house effect, ozone depletion, and political/human rights violations. Without the world watching through modern communications technologies such as television and fax machines, the leaders of Eastern Europe would probably have been able to crush growing dissent in the 1980s, and the "iron curtain" would likely still exist. These technologies, along with newer ones such as e-mail and the internet, also played a key role in organizing the opposition which prevented the implementation of the MAI in the spring of 1998.

At present, however, the destructive side of globalization, that is, growing control by trans-national corporations and the elimination of unique cultures, languages, and communities, seems to be winning. Under the seductive blandishments of liberal, capitalist ideology, scientific knowledge, and modern technology, we are witnessing the global spread of many of the industrialized world's worst political, economic, social, and environmental practices, especially individualistic consumer-culture. Many are applauding the economic transformation of such places as Malaysia, Singapore, Taiwan, and China, seemingly blissfully unaware that long-term, consumption-oriented styles of living are unsustainable globally. Unfortunately, very little is often said by western leaders when these countries ignore positive liberal qualities such as tolerance, freedom of expression and association, and equality.

But then who are Canadians to be critical of the global spread of the consumer-driven life-style, one few of them would be willing to forsake, to which many are addicted, and upon which they rely? Most welcome, or at least shop at, the trans-national owned and/or driven mega-malls and mega-stores such as Costco, Wal-Mart, and Home Depot because of the "value" they offer, even as they wreak havoc with local business and infrastructure, and rob small communities of their "capital." Few are willing to forego the short-term "benefits" of materialistic consumption for the long-term health of their communities. Besides, many rationalize, even if they as individuals were to change their consumption-oriented ways, the policies of the country's governments and elites would still continue to favour the forces of globalization rather than those of local communities, industries, and businesses. And as individuals, most Canadians fear being "left behind."

It is appropriate to lament the willingness not only of Canada's leaders and elites but also of each of us to permit the demise of the country's unique communities and environments by ceding control over our way of life to outside, global, economic interests. If Canada's identity as a sovereign state is indeed built upon the country's varied communities and regions, and if these continue to lose their unique character and identity, Canada itself will not survive. There will be little incentive or reason for people across the northern half of North America to call themselves Canadian. Quebec separatists have already recognized how the modern, liberal dream threatens unique cultures, although they are naive in their hope that political independence alone will help them preserve their cultural identity. As they will discover if they achieve independence, it is difficult to maintain a cohesive and sovereign state in today's globalizing environment, perhaps even impossible.

But, as Grant noted, lamenting is not despairing. A lament, while it marks the end of one thing, also announces the start of something new. In the last decade or so, all across the planet, increasing numbers of people are turning to what has been called "grassroots democracy," taking up numerous local causes, whether they be the protection of community habitats, the quality of their children's schools, recreation needs, levels of taxation, infrastructure in their communities, crime in their neighbourhoods, development projects, etc. Despite, or perhaps because of, trans-national corporate globalism, people are fighting back to fulfil what Spretnak calls a basic need, the desire to experience a sense of place and to make their natural and man-made environments safe and healthy places to live. As the "global" spreads, the "local" fights back.

It is unclear, however, despite such achievements as stalling the MAI, if "grassroots" movements will carry enough influence to give people control over their communities and their every-day lives. If we accept Harris' notion of Canada as an archipel-ago, then it is likely that the destruction of the identity of the islands will inevitably result in the loss of Canada. It is on the "islands," therefore, that the fight to save Canada will also be won or lost.

NOTES

1 The free trade deal did not substantially change Canada's relationship with the United States, the country which absorbs 80% of Canada's trade. By 1989, tariffs were either non-existent or very low on most items crossing the border. The significance of the deal lies in its sym-bolic completion of a process as old as this country.

2 The recent phenomenon of "just in time" production in smaller plants reinforces, even amplifies, the bond of (local) production units to the large, corporate structures to which they supply parts.

3 For a full treatment of the reluctance of governments to tackle this question, see Linda McQuaig's *The Cult of Impotence: Selling the Myth of Powerlessness in the Global Economy* (1998).

2

CANADA: THE NATION

The rights of the minority must be
protected, and the rich are always fewer
in number than the poor.
— Sir John A. Macdonald

When George Grant, in his lament more than thirty years ago, saw Diefenbaker as the last hope for Canadian sovereignty, he did not overlook the fact that the near impossibility of establishing and maintaining a sovereign Canadian state was built into its ideological and constitutional foundation. Diefenbaker was simply the latest incarnation of the ideals of the founders of Canada, those men who envisioned a modern, liberal, industrial, capitalist state across the northern half of North America, from the Atlantic to the Pacific, distinct from, and even an alternative to, the United States of America. Like Diefenbaker ninety years later, they had not considered that acceptance of the ideology which had shaped the United States would lead to the creation of a country and way of life based on similar values. Thus, for Grant, Diefenbaker's defeat was not so much a turning point as the seal of the victory of liberalism in Canada.

Indeed, for Canada's founding fathers, there was no real debate about the implementation of liberal, capitalist, industrial ideals. From their point of view, the real problems, even obstacles, in the way of building a new country were not ideological. Geography was obviously a serious difficulty, but it could be overcome. No, the more worrisome issue was the seeming lack of enthusiasm for confederation among Britain's North American colonies on July 1, 1867, except in Ontario and in isolated pockets in the Maritimes. Quebec, then as now, under the influence of conservative, nationalist sentiments, was uncertain about the benefits of belonging to a state in which non-francophones were an ever-expanding majority. Natives were not considered or consulted, New Brunswickers and Nova Scotians were largely suspicious, and Newfoundland and Prince Edward Island rejected confederation by remaining British colonies, the former waiting until 1949 to join Canada. West of the Great Lakes, except for a few Europeans who had moved to the Red River area in the early nineteenth century because of the fur trade and Lord Selkirk's immigration schemes, and for a few thousand British settlers on the west coast, there was little consideration given to creating a country from the Atlantic to the Pacific.

In truth, most of the reasons for Canada's creation were negative and reactive. The primary reason for confederation was the proximity of the aggressively expansionist United States. After the Revolution of 1775,[1] the United States had slowly filled the mid-west, then the southwest, and finally the far west. By the mid-nineteenth century, expansive Yankee eyes were cast northward at a handful of British colonies, all but one in the eastern half of the continent. The citizens of these British colonies, made up predominantly of English, Irish, and French descendants, were none too eager to be swallowed up by Yankee democracy which many of them characterized as lawless and violent. The American civil war, between 1861 and 1865, did nothing to enhance this image. Many British North Americans sympathized with the south in its stand against a centralizing federal United States' government.

The second reason for Canadian confederation was Britain's desire to divest itself of the cost of running its relatively stable colonies with dominant white populations. Granting these colonies self-governing status would mean the continuation of trade connections but would save the costs of administration and defence. The American Revolution had demonstrated to British leaders what could happen when colonies were held in check too long.

A third factor in the creation of Canada was the problem of French Canada. In 1841, the British government had joined Lower and Upper Canada into the United Province of Canada, administratively dividing it into French-dominant Canada East and English-dominant Canada West. Political stalemate between the French and English in the Province of Canada over the next two decades had led political leaders from both sides to conclude that confederation and splitting the colony into the provinces of Ontario and Quebec was the best solution for all concerned. Believing that this option guaranteed strong provincial rights, French Canadian leaders chose this option. Canadian federalism was seen as better for Quebec than isolated independence in a dominant Anglophone continent or union with the United States.

Despite the lack of popular enthusiasm at Canada's birth, there were nonetheless avid boosters, especially among the old colonial leaders and businessmen who had been converted to the emerging liberal, nationalist, industrial, capitalist vision that was sweeping Europe and the United States in the first half of the nineteenth century. These men envisioned a vast state in the northern half of North America, connected by railways and telegraphs. Their conception had been reinforced by no fewer than four scientific and geological surveys in the 1850s which had confirmed that the lands west of the Great Lakes contained boundless resources of timber, minerals, and grain-growing prairie soils, all of which would provide the raw material for an unlimited range of industrial goods to be produced in the emerging, manufacturing, central-Canadian heartland. The gold rush of 1858 in New Caledonia (soon to be named British Columbia) merely extended the vision to the Pacific. Enthusiasts such as the essayist, Henry Youle Hind (in the 1860s), reckoned that, among the industrializing, capitalist nations of the western world, Canada had potential second to none:

> In eighty years, [Canada's British colonies have] . . . increased tenfold, not only in population but in wealth; they have attained to a point of power that more than equals that of the united colonies when they were separated from the mother country. They have, by means of canals, made their great rivers and remote inland seas accessible to the shipping of Europe; they have constructed a system of railroads far surpassing those of some European powers; they have established an educational system which is behind none in the old or new world; they have developed vast agricultural and inexhaustible mineral resources; they have done enough, in short, to indicate a magnificent future — enough to point to a progress which shall place the provinces, within the days of many now living, on a level with Great Britain herself, in population, in wealth, and in power.

This was no modest vision. Remarkably, when he wrote these words, there was no serious challenge to Britain's global industrial and military dominance.

To fulfil its vision of an integrated economic and political union after achieving status as an independent colony in 1867,[2] the new government of Canada, led by its cagey Prime Minister, John A. Macdonald, pursued three major objectives. The first was the acquisition of Rupert's Land (essentially the prairies and northern regions) from the Hudson's Bay Company, finalized in 1870, but only after a major Métis rebellion led by Louis Riel. The second was obtaining British Columbia from Britain in 1871, after British Columbians had been promised a rail connection in ten years and the elimination of its colonial debt. The Dominion now was truly "from sea to sea." The third objective was the railroad from the Atlantic to the Pacific, started in the 1870s, and completed in 1885, but only after a second Métis rebellion. When Riel was hanged in 1886, more was lost for the Natives and the Métis than Riel's life. They had been washed aside by the dominant Anglo-French tide.

The economic vision underlying these objectives was beautiful in its simplicity. Canada's economy would be a unified system, with each region's local autonomy being replaced by its integration into the centre. The Montreal/Toronto industrial heartland would be fed by resources from the hinterlands, whether fish, timber, and minerals from the Maritimes, British Columbia, Northern Quebec, and Northern Ontario, or grain from the prairies. Ottawa would impose tariffs on imports to establish and expand this system, both to protect the burgeoning central Canadian industries from foreign competition and to force the regions outside of the centre to buy its products. This system marked the beginning of a regional disparity which still characterizes Canada. The development of a sense of Canadian unity and identity would have to overcome this obvious economic weighting by the federal government and central Canadian business leaders.

After the Pacific Scandal of 1873, the new Liberal government led by Alexander MacKenzie raised tariffs even higher, continued building railroads (albeit at a slower pace), and negotiated treaties with prairie Natives so that white settlers could move into these otherwise "unused lands" and properly exploit prairie soils to become the bread basket for Canada. The Liberals' policies differed little from those of Macdonald's Conservatives, a pattern of succession which essentially has never been broken. The die had been cast. A pragmatic liberalism would guide Canada for the next one hundred and thirty years.

John A. Macdonald regained office in 1878 on the basis of his famous National Policy which, like previous colonial and national economic policies, set a uniformly high tariff on imports to protect a burgeoning Canadian secondary industry, promised a faster pace in completing the trans-continental railway, and actively pursued immigration as a nation-building tool. Macdonald explained that the policy would ". . . benefit and foster the agricultural, the mining, the manufacturing and other interests of the Dominion [and] will encourage an active interprovincial trade." He added, "Formerly, we were a number of Provinces with little trade with each other . . . and it is of the greatest importance that we should be allied together." Instead of the Maritimes looking to the United States or England for trade, they would look to Ontario and Quebec, ". . . sending their products west, and receiving the products of Quebec and Ontario in exchange." The National Policy would maintain its essential form until the Depression of the 1930s.

One other noteworthy element of the policy, despite its imposition of a uniform rate of tariffs, was its long term commitment to free trade, the sacred cow of nineteenth-century liberalism. Macdonald, while agreeing in principle with free traders such as Goldwyn Smith, disagreed with their call for an immediate end to tariff protection and for economic union with the United States. Instead, because of his fears of economic domination by the United States, Macdonald argued that the National Policy would protect Canada's industry in the short term. In the long term, such protection would enable Canada to move ". . . in the direction of a reciprocity of tariffs with our neighbours, [and] eventually, a reciprocity of trade."

When the Liberal Party of Wilfrid Laurier took the reins of control from 1896-1911, it maintained the National Policy, built another transcontinental railroad to foster the east-west connection, encouraged the biggest wave of immigration to the prairies this country has ever seen, and fostered foreign investment to industrialize Canada's centre. By 1911, Canada's urban population had almost equalled its rural population in real numbers. Laurier is famous for his prediction that the twentieth would be "Canada's century," by which he meant that Canada would become one of the world's elite industrial, capitalist nations. However, he misjudged the Canadian business and industrial sectors' lack of willingness to compete internationally without tariff protection. When he proposed free trade in 1910, these sectors allied themselves with the Conservative Party to defeat him at the polls, not because his opponents believed that free trade was wrong in the long term, but because they felt that the country was not ready for it.

Nonetheless, by this time, the vision of a Canada integrated by means of the National Policy had already defined Canada's economy. As historian T. W. Acheson has noted, in the last two decades of the nineteenth century, the maritime provinces saw many of their key industries (textiles, timber and shipbuilding, manufacturing, sugar refining, iron, and steel) either disappear or bought up by capital from outside the region, largely from Britain and from the emerging Canadian metropolitan regions of Toronto and Montreal. By 1910, he notes, the Maritimes had lost control over their financial destiny as well as their previously dominant trading focus with Britain and the United States. This was just as Macdonald had proposed, but the benefits which he had promised never materialized. The twentieth has certainly not been the "Maritimes' century." The dream of a prosperous, liberal nation from sea to sea has not yet delivered for this region, which has been plagued by chronic depression and unemployment.

The same loss of regional and local control was true for the prairies and for British Columbia, where freight policies, trade relations, land policies, interest rates, and economic/industrial activity had redirected the economy to the needs of central Canada. In contrast to the Maritimes, however, the people of these regions have experienced relative wealth because of a continued abundance of resources deemed useful by the industrial centre, whether for trade or for manufacture. But make no mistake about it, that wealth too has been dependent on outside control and direction. Outsiders have provided the bulk of the capital to extract and market resources, and have supplied the majority of manufactured goods for everyday life.

What has been true for the regions, however, has also been true for the centre. Canada's commitment to liberal values doomed its hopes for economic independence right from the start. Even though governments attempted to protect Canadian business and industry by tariffs, money was still needed to develop Canada's economy. Investment funds necessary for capital and industrial development do not arise in a vacuum. They come from those who have them, and, thus, newly industrializing countries inevitably find themselves reliant on outside capital investment for development. In the case of Canada, the desire to create a large east-west empire over an extremely difficult geography contributed to the need for far more outside capital than would be required by geographically smaller countries or if its development patterns had been on a smaller and more locally diversified scale.

This reality provided a wonderful window of opportunity for American investors. Despite legislating tariffs to restrict the flow of imports into Canada, Canadian governments permitted the free flow of foreign capital into its economy, thereby allowing non-Canadian industrialists and capitalists an alternative way to profit from emerging Canadian markets and from the country's myriad resources. By 1922, American foreign investment capital exceeded that from all other sources, rising to over 60% by 1930. Furthermore, American branch-plants, as in the automobile industry (whose productive value, one analyst claimed at the time, exceeded that of any other industry), set up by Americans to bypass the tariff wall, became a dominant force in Canada's manufacturing industries. In 1918, there were 466 United States' branch plants in Canada; 641 more would be added in the next twelve years. Although the National Policy was successful in establishing a strong Canadian industrial base, the method that it used, namely, that of tariff protection, failed to do what it was designed for, namely, to prevent control by outside economic and industrial forces.

The change to an industrial society radically altered the way

Canadians lived. By the 1920s, just over fifty percent of Canadians lived in towns and cities. Fewer people farmed, while more worked in white collar and service industries. Wheat farming, which because of automation was employing ever smaller numbers of workers, boomed because of the loss to Europe of Russia's production after the 1917 Bolshevik revolution. Canada's pulp and paper industry was second to none, providing over 60% of world production by 1929 (one-third owned by United States' investors). Canada's natural resources were seen as limitless, capable of providing Canadians with an infinitely expanding good life. Like their American counterparts, Canadians took to the automobile, listened to radios, attended movies, filled their homes with appliances, bought on credit, invested in the stock market, and so forth. Canada's resources were not only helping Canada's industries to boom but were providing raw materials to other countries as well. Modernity and the good life seemed synonymous. "Primitive" Canada was fading into memory.

The crash of western economies in 1929 underscored the fragility of this new liberal, industrial, capitalist way of life. Unlike most scourges in the history of humanity, the Depression of the 1930s was not a natural but a man-made disaster. Throughout the western world, overproduction, a frenzy of irresponsible and uncontrolled corporate mergers, an unregulated and overheated stock market, a precarious international trading system, and flawed monetary arrangements began undermining consumer confidence to produce an economic depression that lasted a decade.

Like people in Europe and the United States, countless Canadians lost their jobs, their savings, and their self-respect. Government remedies were of little avail. Western leaders, following traditional liberal practice, prayed that the economic and industrial order which they had spent the last hundred years constructing would fix itself. But their faith in a self-regulating market place was not rewarded. Canadian Prime Ministers, Mackenzie King, R. B. Bennett, and King again, muddled through. In 1938, King appointed the Rowell-Sirois Commission to investigate the causes of the Depression and to recommend solutions. The Commission reported in 1940, after World War II had started and the Depression was lifting. It noted:

> For upwards of thirty years external influences and technical changes had played favourably upon Canada's resources and produced an era of almost unbroken expansion and prosperity. The Canadian economy had become delicately geared to the increasing foreign markets for foodstuffs, newsprint, lumber, and minerals. For the production of these commodities, a large and expensive transportation system was built and huge amounts invested in power projects, processing plants, implements, and machines. Much of the capital required for the provision of this immense equipment was borrowed from other countries. The application of this capital and of advanced techniques to virgin resources became the principal basis of our economic life. It involved a narrow specialization in the production of a few export staples, heavy fixed charges, and a precarious dependence upon the commercial policies of other countries.

> As long as the conditions of international trade were favourable, specialization yielded a high standard of living. Our social and economic institutions became closely related to the nature of the economy and rested on the condition of continuous expansion. When the bases for progress along the old lines disappeared and the full force of the world depression fell upon our specialized exports, the problems of adjustment were extremely difficult. Canada's political, pub-

lic finance, and economic organizations were not adapted to deal with sharp and prolonged economic reverses. . . .

The policies of Western settlement, all-Canadian transportation, and industrialization by protective tariffs had been designed to promote, and to function under the influences of, expansion. The success of the whole scheme depended upon the availability of extensive virgin resources and expanding foreign markets. In 1930, when the external influences became extremely unfavourable and the supply of new land suitable for agriculture had been virtually exhausted, the old policies became largely negative. [T]he nation's prosperity could no longer be maintained simply by settling immigrants and subsidizing the construction of new railways.

The Commission sent a clear message that Canada's reliance on resource industries to subsidize secondary industries, largely controlled by non-Canadians, its dependence on foreign trade to provide the wealth necessary for the lifestyle to which Canadians were increasingly becoming accustomed, and its commitment to continuous growth and expansion had created an economy vulnerable to forces largely beyond the control of Canadians and their governments.

During World War II, the federal government assumed virtual control of the country and of its economy by passing the War Measures Act, creating the Wartime Industries Control Board and hundreds of Crown Corporations, and agreeing to collective bargaining rights for labour. Full employment was reached by 1943, including women who had entered the workforce in record numbers in non-traditional female jobs.

Whether or not this interventionist approach would have worked in the long term, and whether or not it would have been deemed dictatorial in a democratic society is unknown. Instead, after World War II, the elite which had ruled Canada through the Depression and the world war, paid little attention to the findings of the Commission and the federal government's experience of managing the economy during the war, and simply modified the liberal philosophy which had guided it in the past. For many of this elite, a hands-on approach to economic matters might have been appropriate for war-time emergencies, but in the cold war atmosphere of the day, such an approach smacked of socialism, and socialism was a "mere hop, skip, and jump from communism." For all of its faults, liberal, capitalist ideals were still held by most to be appropriate for economic and political life. They would be *made* to work, considering the alternative.

Furthermore, the government had to deal with popular expectations. Canadian workers had tasted full employment during the war and, quite legitimately, were anxious not to revert to the distress of the Depression. The American ideological and propaganda machine was in full gear, promising North Americans a brave new consumer future, with sleek cars, televisions, vacations, gadgets, and appliances that would not only take the drudgery out of everyday life but provide untold delights. The Mackenzie King Liberals, skilled at getting re-elected, concluded that the easiest, most sure-fire way to provide Canadians with this sparkling consumer future was to abandon war-time control over the economy and to revert to pre-war economic practices which had worked previously, with modifications to avoid repeating the breakdowns of the 1930s.

The 1945 "White Paper on Employment and Income" provided the framework for the direction which the Mackenzie King government, under the direction of the expatriate American, C.D. Howe, would take the economy. Essentially, the government would arrange a new social contract among key sectors of society (hereafter referred to as the post-war state) and would redefine the relationship among three key parties in Canada's economy: 1. Governments (federal and provincial), 2. business and industry, and 3. labour.

The federal government would grant business and industry subsidies and tax breaks, while provincial governments would be equally generous in providing the corporate sector with new roads, crown lands (long-term leases), and social and health services. This generosity, it was believed, would spur business and industry to invest in Canada's resources and to provide both the technological expertise for modern industry and the accompanying high-paying jobs to give post-war Canadians the high standard of living which they were expecting. The price that business and industry would have to pay for government largesse involved the third party, labour. Ottawa guaranteed labour's newly gained right to collective bargaining as well as the right to strike in negotiating contracts with business and industry.

The fact that both federal and provincial governments pledged to implement social legislation and wide-ranging welfare benefits to protect citizens in tough economic times made the deal palatable to both business and labour. Alvin Finkel has argued that the post-war state with its welfare benefits was created only after consultation with the country's business and industrial leaders, who feared that mechanization, unemployment, poverty, and inadequate health care raised the spectre of working class revolt. The post-war state (sometimes called the "welfare state"[3]), he notes,

> . . . changes nothing that is fundamental about capitalism. While it places a floor on workers' incomes, it leaves unaltered the control of the means of production. Production for

profit and not for use and the reduction of labour to an extension of the machines it operates for the benefit of capital remain the goals of the economic system. There can be little doubt that government social programs do serve the function of legitimizing the system by making it appear that the worst aspects of laissez-faire have been compensated.

The post-war state, thus, had a conservative purpose. Ironically, recent efforts to dismantle the post-war state in the name of capitalist free enterprise may actually put capitalism at risk by unleashing the social tensions which those who created the post-war state sought to control.

After the war, with slight modifications to the basic liberal approach, the new "social contract" meant that it was back to business as usual. American corporations invested in Canada at a dizzying rate, bringing their technology to pillage the forests and mines of the hinterlands, investing in secondary manufacturing in central Canada, and, generally, providing Canadians with opportunities to make lots of money. In 1946, 35% of Canada's manufacturing was foreign controlled. By 1953, it would be 50%, and 56% by 1957. Even more staggering was the foreign control of Canada's mining industry: 70% by 1957. The downside was that, even as Canadians were making "good money," the profits and dollars flowed out of the country, an amount, Wallace Clement notes, that reached $1,481 billion annually by 1974. For Canadians to maintain the good life, they had to produce ever more for the export market to bring cash into the country. But an enormous amount of cash in the form of profits was also leaving.

Few Canadians seemed to mind. For them, the good life was expanding dramatically: they built bigger houses, bought fancier cars (many families acquired two), and filled their lives with ever more consumer goods. Corporations could afford to be generous with workers. Roads and railways for their benefit were being built at taxpayer's expense. Profits were large, and tax laws were kind. By the mid-sixties, expanded social legislation gave industry and business an even easier ride as the welfare of the work-force fell largely on the shoulders of the tax-paying public rather than on the corporate sector. Lay off a worker, and he/she would collect unemployment insurance. Medicare would take care of health, and free public schooling would provide education, even the technical and scientific training for the workforce required by industry. And, finally, minimal environmental legislation maximized profits. How could the corporate sector be unhappy? Besides, there seemed to be enough money to meet everyone's needs. If the system broke down? Corporations could blame governments and their policies, whether the tax laws, excessive regulation, or the social security network. And then pack up and leave if governments refused to give them even better deals.

The problem that the Rowell-Sirois Commission had clearly articulated in 1940 was magnified. Not only had Canada once again oriented its economy to reliance on the outside world to buy its resources (many of which are non-renewable and will run out eventually, while many of the renewable ones are being harvested more quickly than they can regenerate), it had created a social contract which gave huge tax and infrastructure benefits to the corporate sector, and committed the government to paying workers large sums of money during bad times, when corporations would be unable to meet their commitments to workers, and when revenues to the state would actually be declining. If governments ran short of funds to honour this commitment to the corporate sector and to workers, John

Maynard Keynes' theories were a handy justification for them to borrow money.

The system functioned happily as long as two conditions were met. Firstly, the world would have to continue to covet Canada's resources. Secondly, and more importantly, Canada would have to continue to possess such resources. The first condition has not consistently been the case since 1945. There have been downturns in Canada's economy, largely for the same reasons as reported by the Rowell-Sirois commission, namely, soft international markets for resources coupled with Canada's reliance on external economic forces. Still, governments, until recently, have largely kept their commitment to the corporate sector and to their welfare policies to mitigate the potential impacts of such downturns. But Canadians are reaching an impasse. The cost of providing tax incentives to corporations, of building and maintaining costly infrastructure, and of supporting the social network seems to have expanded beyond the government's ability to pay, partly because the second condition is failing. Canada's fisheries, forests, mines, and agriculture sectors no longer are capable of producing infinite wealth to provide the money for the system — should the world continue to desire its resources. In short, the natural environment cannot afford the post-war state.

The post-war social contract became a problem, thus, not because it was the product of misguided socialistic tendencies of past federal governments as some neo-liberals would have Canadians believe. Rather, it was an adaptation of the fundamental liberal, capitalist direction western economies had been following since the days of Adam Smith and Ricardo. Like all liberal states from the inception of capitalism, the post-war state gave corporations freedom to make huge profits without requiring these *private* entities to concern themselves much with the well-being of their workers or of the natural environment which gave them so much wealth. But unlike the early days of capitalism, when there was no real safety net and workers were at the mercy of capitalists, the post-war state and its taxpayers had committed themselves to picking up the pieces of bad corporate planning by protecting the workers. The post-war state allowed capitalism to thrive without, once again, requiring appropriate corporate responsibility. The country had ignored the lesson of the Rowell-Sirois Commission. Like Canada's pre-Depression economy (especially the 1920s), the post-war system had become too reliant on resource exploitation and outside markets. And it had ignored sustainability and self-reliance.

There is a perversity in liberal capitalism, which Adam Smith had already observed in 1776, in that it requires a rather nebulous quality, "confidence," to remain healthy. Most people usually know enough to stop making purchases if they do not believe that they have reasonable prospects for continued access to sufficient amounts of money to pay their bills and to buy life's necessities. Conventional capitalist wisdom has suggested that a slow but steady rate of growth is the best way to maintain this consumer confidence. No growth, it is said, removes incentives to work and save. On the other hand, rapid growth and inflation may cause panic, as prices rise quickly, labour unrest grows because workers fear they cannot keep pace, and incentives to work and save are jeopardized. The trick, economics gurus declare, is to maintain slow, steady growth which will ensure continued consumer confidence.

This is always easier said than done, as is shown by the continuous series of booms and busts in the history of western capitalism. Following World War II, there was some faith that governments could, through fiscal policies, mitigate the impacts of boom and bust periods. Inflation and stagnation, it was argued, could be controlled by tightening or loosening the money supply and by raising or lowering interest rates. One of the acknowledged consequences of this control of the money supply would be varying levels of unemployment; with a tighter money supply and higher interest rates, there would be less money and fewer jobs. Government borrowing would pick up the slack during the leaner times.

Combined with the social contract of the post-war state, the theory seemed to work. For the first few decades after the war, Canadians were lulled into a false sense of security, assuming that the steady progress of expanding wealth since 1945 was the norm, and that questioning this path of economic "progress" was naysaying. Serious problems, however, began to rise in the late 1960s and early 1970s, as inflation and unemployment, allegedly generated by problems in the United States' economy because of the Vietnam war, suggested that there might be limits to the growth of the international economic order. The United States, the world's dominant economic power, was experiencing inflationary pressure at levels that its economists believed were unacceptable. In 1970, President Richard Nixon's government responded by implementing wage and price controls. Canada followed with controls in 1975. Unfortunately, these policies did not achieve the desired results. There was the expected rise in unemployment, but, contrary to contemporary economic wisdom, inflation continued, prompting a new term, "stagflation." As the American economy went, so did those of the other major industrial economies.

The energy crisis of 1973-1974 exacerbated these trends.

Western governments, including Canada's, began borrowing to pay bills, inflation in the 1970s and early 1980s hit double digits several times, and disillusionment with politicians and economic experts grew. As the Canadian government went ever deeper into the hole to maintain its deal with the corporate sector, its commitment to resource infrastructure, and its guarantee of social services, the folly of tying the country to the international economic order, particularly to the American empire, once more became apparent. The Keynesian post-war social contract was showing grave weakness. By the early 1980s, western governments' annual deficits and national debts had become major problems. Federal borrowing in the 1990s (up to the 1998 budget, anyway) was not to pay for current costs but for interest payments on money borrowed annually since the early 1970s.[4]

Paul Martin's 1998 budget has promised to be the first balanced (or even surplus) one in decades. But it has come with serious costs. It is the result of the victory of a variant of classical liberal ideals, a movement calling itself "neo-conservatism" (as noted in chapter 1, this book will use the more accurate term for this phenomenon, namely, neo-liberalism). Based on the same eighteenth-century liberal foundation as Keynesianism, it urged a return to pre-Keynesian liberalism. It asserted that the "welfare states" created by western democracies after World War II had become too costly and inefficient. Labour had become too greedy, workers too lazy, and the government too large. It called for a return to so-called laissez-faire economics, free enterprise, and self-reliance, as well as for government downsizing and an end to government regulations which it said were strangling business and personal initiative. The American economist, Milton Friedman, advocated a peculiar theory which he called "supply-side economics" where lower taxes and a deregulated industrial and business environment would stimulate investment and corporate growth which, in turn, would produce more goods, money, and tax revenue, and would provide a larger number of jobs. Governments, he said, should allow the corporate sector to operate with virtually no interference.[5] This so-called hands-off approach, the theory claimed, would allow the private sector to generate large profits and an ever-larger pool of capital which would magically find its way to the pockets of lower levels of society, enriching all citizens. Never mind that a similar "unregulated" economic environment in the 1920s had been largely responsible for the Depression of the 1930s. Never mind that economic desperation at that time had led a number of western governments to radical alternatives, the worst of which were those of dictators such as Franco, Mussolini, and especially Hitler. Never mind that the so-called welfare state had demanded too little responsibility of the corporate sector rather than too much.

Throughout western Europe and North America, a liberal civil war broke out, with the neo-liberals attacking labour unions, post-war social welfare legislation, environmental regulations, immigration policies, and anything else which could not produce a "bottom line" that said "profit." Canada's millionaire Prime Minister, Pierre Elliot Trudeau, went on television and told Canadians that they had been too greedy and had to tighten their belts. In 1979, neo-liberal Margaret Thatcher became Prime Minister of Great Britain, followed by the election, in 1980, of neo-liberal Ronald Reagan to the presidency of the United States. Both were committed to versions of supply-side economics and to eliminating what they called the welfare state. In 1984, Canada elected a neo-liberal Prime Minister, the Progressive Conservative Brian Mulroney, whose success as a neo-liberal can be judged by the fact that, in 1998, the political landscape has been overtaken by this ideology. Virtually all federal and provincial parties across Canada are committed to essentially the same economic policies.

Driven by these neo-liberal policies, federal and provincial governments of the past decade or so have attacked the social contract which created the post-war state, deregulating everything from environmental protection laws to union rights to airline and transportation regulations. In the name of fiscal restraint and financial saving, they are privatizing profitable crown corporations and numerous government services. Cultural programs and icons such as the CBC, an institution which some call the modern "transcontinental railway," are being scuttled. Universality in social and medical benefits is being curtailed with user fees and competing private for-profit medical clinics for those who have the money to pay for them. Taxes for big corporations and the wealthy have been reduced, while middle and lower income citizens find themselves saddled increasingly with ever higher fees, sales taxes, income taxes, and other charges. The unemployed and welfare recipients are finding benefits reduced, even eliminated. Free trade agreements and tariff reductions are allowing revenues from exports to increase dramatically, benefitting primarily the corporate sector which produces them but doing little for the outrageously high number of people who are unemployed, especially those under the age of twenty-five. Make no mistake about it, the pursuit of these regressive policies has allowed Mr. Martin to reduce government spending in the mid-1990s and to produce his balanced budget of 1998.

While such measures were undertaken to decrease government deficits and debt and to encourage more wealth by freeing the private sector to do what it allegedly does best, namely, make lots of money for everyone, the benefits have not been distributed evenly among the rest of the population. Throughout the 1990s, because exports have continually exceeded imports, economists and government officials have insisted that Canada's "economy" was "booming." But ask average Canadians if they agree, and they will tell you what survey after survey shows, namely, that the financial position of most Canadians has worsened significantly, and that only the elite and the rich (essentially one and the same) have become richer. One study has noted that inflation-adjusted hourly wages (the manner in which lower income workers are generally paid) in 1997 are below 1973 levels. The decreasing value of the Canadian dollar through the spring and summer of 1998 has opened the floodgates to foreign investment and takeovers, a reality which, because federal governments of the last fifteen years have placed few (even removed) restrictions on investment, will simply exacerbate these trends.

George Grant would not have been surprised. Very little has changed about the way the elite runs this country. Like governments of the 1890s, those of the late 1990s are committed to creating an integrated Canadian industrial economy, along liberal, capitalist lines, an economy which, they believe, will make it a giant among the other industrialized countries. But the post-war social contract under which Canada has operated since 1945 as a means of attaining this end is being forsaken because neo-liberals claim that it is no longer affordable. Instead, Canadians are exhorted to lower their sights and recognize that a market economy driven by the "natural law" of supply and demand is in their long-term best interests. In this "new reality," as Prime Minister Chretien noted on a television "town hall" meeting early in 1997, there will be "winners" and there will be "losers." Unemployment may remain high, but the responsibility for issues such as employment, pensions, and health care should reside more with the individual than with paternalistic governments who have little idea about efficient management or bottom-line budgeting. Somehow our elites have forgotten that, in addition to personal failings, there were systemic reasons for poverty in the Depression of the 1930s. That is just as true today. Neo-liberalism seems driven more by ideology than common sense. One has to wonder how many well-researched and scholarly history and economics books the leading advocates of neo-liberalism have read.

By arguing for a global economic battle-ground, where individuals, corporations, and even countries may sink, today's neo-liberals exhibit a Darwinian approach to the liberal dream. Such potential impacts, they say, are the inevitable price of survival in today's competitive, modern, market-driven economy. Corporations should be free to move to where they can find the best deal, that is, countries where there are few environmental restrictions, negligible labour legislation, and low labour costs. Borders should be irrelevant; homogenization of products and economies is desirable. Their allies in the World Bank, the IMF, and the World Trade Organization, directed by the world's leading profit-oriented banks and corporations, are telling nations how to manage their budgets, administer their social programs, and build their infrastructure, with little or no regard for indigenous ways or needs. As Richard Lacayo pointed out in *Time* (Dec. 8, 1997), the "IMF is both a bank of last resort and a fiscal reform school for wayward economies, [a] lever to keep countries in line." When countries "admit their sins," the IMF sends in economists and experts to help them take the straight and narrow road. He points out that "applying to the fund means lost economic sovereignty. The fund's recommendations also mean pain for the poor and working class when governments accept the fund's austere recommendations." The liberal, industrial model has become the law which must be obeyed. With such control and direction by financial elites, the global economy is hardly a free-market system. And nobody is required to take responsibility for consequences, because the forces of globalization are "natural," the inevitable unfolding of history. Citizen participation in government, that "something" which has traditionally been called democracy, no longer has value because people are told they no longer have any power or control over their lives and must bow to inevitable destiny.

Little was learned from the Depression or the Rowell-Sirois Commission. Even among the critics of globalization and free trade, there is no clear view of what the Depression actually should have taught Canadians. Stephen McBride and John Shields, for example, in *Dismantling a Nation,* argue that the Keynesian, post-war state strengthened Canadians' pride in and loyalty to their country by setting up programs to overcome regional disparity and by creating a social safety net so that all citizens would have equal access to essential health and welfare programs. By dismantling both the equalization programs and the social welfare system, by scuttling the railway networks, by privatizing government functions, or by impoverishing the CBC, they argue, neo-liberals are in effect "dismantling the nation" by undoing the bonds that united the country. Free trade agreements restrict the federal government's ability to act in the country's interest by placing Canada's economic destiny in the hands of international, global, market forces and corporations.[6]

While much of what they say is valid, they do not go far enough. There is little doubt that neo-liberal, trans-national corporatism is weakening Canada's sovereignty, but the reason for the erosion of sovereignty and the loss of pride in the country is far more complex than the recent replacement of Keynesianism by neo-liberalism. In fact, as Wallace Clement has noted, the policies of the Canadian state have always been focussed on "reinforcing these dominant capitalists [who] back winners, whatever their nationality, [whose] interests are inextricably bound to the international system of commerce." The weakness of McBride and Shields' argument, indeed of liberalism generally, whether neo-Keynesian or neo-liberal, is that, like Marxism, it defines the world primarily in economic terms. By arguing that Keynesian economic policies are capable of creating national pride, as if wealth distribution defines a country's self-image, McBride and Shields are unwittingly accepting the premises of those whom they so passionately oppose, those whom they see destroying the country they love.

By blaming neo-liberals for the dismantling of Canada, neo-Keynesians are missing a key point that Grant raised back in the 1960s, namely, that Canada's loss of sovereignty was the result of the very Liberal Party policies which were creating the welfare state whose loss neo-Keynesians such as Shields, McBride, Barlow, Clarke, and McQuaig are fighting. They have failed to understand Grant's central thesis: by adopting the liberal world-view, he said, Canadians have lost control over the fate of their country. He knew that sporadic outbursts of public spirit, whether in such events as Expo 67, international hockey victories, or royal weddings, had little impact on the overall process of disintegration. The Meech Lake and Charlottetown

Accords and the latest Quebec referendum briefly galvanized public attention about the country's future, but constitutional change alone will not, can not, solve Canada's underlying problems. Constitutions do not a country make. The control by the liberal, corporate, political, and communications elite, which Grant blamed for the defeat of Canadian nationalism is still the reality. Indeed, this control is beyond what Grant had described thirty years ago, and it will not be undone until Canadians begin to understand and then fight against the assumptions which underlie it.

The inability of Canada to maintain its sovereignty is really the failure of the Canadian people and their governments to have the insight or intestinal fortitude to stand up to its liberal elite and to maintain the fragile historic linkages among the unique "islands" of the archipelago, the ties which overcame geographic obstacles to make Canada.

Quebec nationalists were among the first in Canada to recognize this threat of liberalism's homogenizing power. Rene Levesque, for example, in 1965, stated:

We are *Quebecois.*

What that means first and foremost . . . is that we are attached to this one corner of the earth where we can be completely ourselves: this Quebec, the only place where we have the unmistakable feeling that here we can be really at home.

Being ourselves is essentially a matter of keeping and developing a personality that has survived for three and a half centuries.

Until recently . . . we enjoyed the protection of a certain degree of isolation. We lived a relatively sheltered life in a rural society.

Our traditional society . . . in which many of us grew up in a way that we thought could, with care, be preserved indefinitely; that "quaint old" society has gone.

Today, most of us are city dwellers, wage earners, tenants. The standards of parish, village, and farm have been splintered. The automobile and the airplane take us "outside" in a way we never could have imagined thirty years ago. . . . Radio and films, and now television, have opened for us a window onto everything that goes on throughout the world: the events — and ideas too — of all humanity invade our homes day after day.

In a world where, in so many fields, the only stable law seems to have become that of perpetual change, where our old certainties are crumbling one after the other, we find ourselves swept along helplessly by irresistible currents.

. . . we must secure once and for all . . . the safety of our collective "personality" . . . in Quebec — the only true fatherland left us by events.

He recognized that separation from Canada would not magically enable French-speaking Quebecers to protect their culture and way of life, but he believed that, with separation, they had a better chance to fight the homogenizing drive of modernity and to determine a future which would reflect their own aspirations than they would under the liberal vision of his federalist counterpart, Pierre Trudeau. Unfortunately, separation will not bring about Levesque's ideal world for the Quebecois. Quebec's problem is both the problem of Canada as a whole and of its regions: uniqueness in the liberal environment of North America may be impossible. With the spread of modern liberal, industrial values, the glue needed to hold unique societies together is losing its grip. And the globalization of these values is making the maintenance of such societies ever more difficult.

The threat to the archipelago, to the country's future, stems not only from the liberal values which dominate the mindsets of the country's elites and of its central institutions. The islands, that is, the country's regions, cities, municipalities, towns, villages, and settlements are driven and dominated by the same liberal dream. Since 1867, the regions have been competing with the federal/national elites for the same slices of the liberal pie, and no leaders from either side have effectively addressed the central question, namely, the premises of liberal ideology. Canadians are in danger of losing their country, and the archipelago is in danger of becoming a series of disconnected islands.

NOTES

1 The actual revolt and fighting started in 1775. The official Declaration of Independence was on July 4, 1776.

2 We must not forget that the British North America Act did not give Canada outright independence. The British Parliament merely created a self-governing colony. Independence would be achieved in 1931 with the Statute of Westminster, although the "patriation" of Canada's constitution would not occur until 1982.

3 The term "welfare state" is a misnomer because it implies a state primarily oriented to the welfare of its citizens. The intent, as Finkel notes, was to save capitalism and not to create some kind of socialist state where political and economic control would devolve to the people, through their governments, and away from the corporate and political elites.

4 Ironically, and unfortunately, borrowing had become necessary for interest on loans because the government's own Bank of Canada set interest rates at astronomically high rates.

5 As Linda McQuaig has pointed out in *The Cult of Impotence,* there was a major exception to this principle of non-interference, namely, the control of inflation. As she notes, the high interest-rate policies of western governments since the late 1970s have illustrated how neo-liberalism is anything but laissez-faire. People everywhere have been conned into believing that the neo-liberal dominance of economics and governments is simply a natural unfolding of the laws of economics. It's not. Those with large amounts of money have been the primary beneficiaries of this theory and of the politics it has spawned.

6 In July 1998, the federal Liberals retreated from imposing an earlier ban on the Ethyl Corporation of Richmond, Virginia of their gasoline additive MMT, a product which allegedly interferes with computerized emission control systems on some cars and poses a significant health hazard. The product is banned in a number of US states (California, for example). The Liberals, in the face of a $250 million NAFTA-based lawsuit, supposedly will pay Ethyl $13 million in exchange for the company dropping its suit.

3

LIFE IN CANADA'S REGIONS

The crash of '29 rocked the world but registered as a
ripple in Cape Breton, where it takes a while for the
depression to sink in because it had already been
going on for so long. Besides, it is widely believed
that Nova Scotia's catastrophe occurred in 1867 with
Confederation. Anything since then has just been an
aftershock.

— Ann-Marie MacDonald, *Fall on Your Knees*

Because of Canada's scattered settlement patterns and its far-
flung geography, it is not surprising that its people have formed
strong attachments to their regions. And given the variation of
resources, economic activities, climates, cultural patterns, and
histories of regions across the country, it is also not unexpected
that tensions exist not only among these regions but also
between them and Canada's central, federal institutions. The
nature, form, and content of these tensions, however, are historically conditioned, the product of the liberal, industrial,

technological, capitalist drive that has dominated Canada since 1867, and which created an economic system which by its design benefited certain parts of the country more than others.[1]

It was the vision of Sir John A. Macdonald and the other "fathers" (there were no women) of confederation that the country's ultimate authority and power should be in the hands of its federal government. A strongly centralized state would guide the creation of a liberal, modern, progressive, industrial country. Historian W.L. Morton notes that

> [Confederation] rested on the explicit subordination of local powers to central, of the state, and of the province, to the nation. [I]t did not rest on the principle of popular sovereignty. On the contrary, it rested on the traditional concept of allegiance to the Crown in which was vested the right and power to govern.
>
> . . . the powers given to the provinces were merely local and private in nature. They were subordinate governments in both appearance and in fact. They had no great tasks to perform and were given no great powers.

In fact, he concludes, the system made ". . . no more provision for local government than was necessary to obtain assent to Confederation from the colonial legislatures." The federal government would speak for the nation as a whole, give the provinces limited powers in areas of strictly provincial concern, reserve the right to disallow provincial legislation, tax by whatever means it felt necessary, and guarantee the duality of French and English culture throughout the country (a goal never clearly defined or implemented). As Macdonald said, "If the Confederation goes on, you, if spared the ordinary age of man, will see both local parliaments and governments absorbed in the general power. This is as plain to me as if I saw it accomplished." The liberal state would be created, and then dominated, by central, federal power; regions and provinces would be subordinate.

This push to the centralization of power in Canada and the subordination of regions and provinces has dominated Canada's history since confederation. It has had two main consequences. The first has been the rise of strong regional movements protesting the power of the political and economic elites which dominate Ottawa and the central government. Such movements have consistently called for recasting the balance of power, although they have seldom dealt with the fundamental values underpinning the Canadian way of life. Rather, they have been concerned more with who gets and distributes the spoils of liberal, capitalist development.

The second has been its impact on everyday life. As noted in the previous chapter, Canada's economic integration has essentially meant that all regions, and, hence, all Canadians, have been forced to orient the patterns of their everyday lives to those dictated by the policies and practices of the central government and the liberal elites which support them. This forced integration and orientation of peoples' routine daily activities has resulted in a cross-Canada homogenization of everyday life, whether in the areas of labour, housing, leisure, or consumption patterns (even though amounts of wealth have varied sharply from one part of the country to the next). In particular, the creation of a capitalist, liberal economic system has forced most people to live in suburban contexts, along with its accompanying environmental, economic, political, social, and personal baggage.

REGIONAL PROTEST MOVEMENTS

Right from the beginning, Canada's provincial leaders fought the system of forced subordination to federal power. A tug of war between the two levels of government was already in full swing as early as 1872, led by Ontario Premier, Oliver Mowat, often called the "father of the provincial rights movement in Canada." He argued for the "compact-theory of confederation," which asserted that, rather than creating a powerful central state, confederation had created a union of separate and equal colonies. The powers given to the provinces in the BNA Act, he believed, limited as they were, had created in the provinces structures of government paralleling those of the federal government, making the governments equal and similar, not subordinate. In 1883, he won a major battle for provincial rights in the British Privy Council over an issue that hardly seemed to be a serious challenge to federal power, namely, the right of provinces to license taverns.

The same principle led W.S. Fielding, Premier of Nova Scotia, in 1886, to drive through his legislature a motion for the secession of the Maritime provinces from Canada. The idea of leaving Canada, driven by the Maritimes' faltering economy, in no small measure a product of the National Policy (see chapter 2), was not accepted by fellow-Maritimers in New Brunswick or Prince Edward Island and, consequently, faded within a year, shortly after a federal election returned a vast majority of con-federationists from the Maritimes. The movement did, however, reflect strong Maritimes' feelings about how confederation seemed to benefit only limited central Canadian interests, a notion that would resurface politically in the 1920s, but has remained part of popular feeling till the present.

In 1887, Quebec elected a strong provincial-rights premier, Honoré Mercier. On the heels of the Riel problem and its perceived threat to French-Canadian interests across the country, he called Canada's first interprovincial conference, attended by Premiers from five of the seven provinces (British Columbia and PEI did not attend because they had provincial governments sympathetic to Prime Minister Macdonald and did not wish to embarrass him). The conference unanimously endorsed resolutions supporting Mowat's compact-theory of confederation, bigger federal subsidies to the provinces, elimination of federal power to disallow provincial legislation, and Senate Reform.

On the west coast, problems with Ottawa surfaced even before British Columbia joined confederation. It took four years of wheeling and dealing, the promise of financial incentives, and the offer of a transcontinental railway link within ten years, before the federal negotiators succeeded in persuading reluctant British Columbia negotiators to unite their colony with Canada in 1871. The railway took fifteen years to complete. The slow pace of construction led to two secession threats, which, along with British Columbia's unceasing demands for better financial arrangements, earned the province the epithet, "spoilt child of confederation."

By the early 1870s, federal actions had also created bad feeling on the prairies. At the time of confederation, this area, from north of the 49th parallel to beyond the Arctic circle, and from the Rockies to Ontario, was owned by a private British corporation, the Hudson's Bay Company (HBC). The Macdonald government quickly negotiated a deal with the HBC to transfer its land to Canada on December 1, 1869. However, before the deal could be signed, the inhabitants of the Red and Assiniboine Rivers area, mostly Natives or Métis, raised objections to this forced annexation of their territory to Canada without their consent. Throughout the winter of 1869-70, their leader, Louis Riel, and the federal government negotiated a deal which led to the creation of Manitoba, the fifth province of Canada (1870). The agreement committed Ottawa and Manitoba to protecting the language and cultural rights of the French-speaking, Catholic majority in Manitoba, as well as guaranteeing the Métis a reservation of 600,000 hectares. The transfer of HBC territory to Canada could finally take place and followed on July 15, 1870.

In the two decades following, Métis settlements were swamped by newcomers, mainly from Ontario. The Métis watched helplessly as the federal government failed to honour its land agreement and to stem the encroachment of non-Manitobans onto their land. In the rest of the former HBC territory, the federal government coerced the Natives into signing treaties, forcing them to cede title and rights to their lands in exchange for reservations and token payments. In the mid-1880s, an uncoordinated and fragmented army of Natives and Métis, led again by Riel, rose up in a last, futile rebellion against federal government policies to extend the trans-continental railway through their remaining lands in what is now Saskatchewan. This time Riel was executed for treason, leaving a legacy of resentment, from both this region (especially from Natives and Métis) and from Quebec, which still has not been fully overcome.[2] Neither the wishes of the residents nor demands for their rights would get in the way of Ottawa's vision for Canada.

With the Natives and Métis no longer impeding progress, the federal government began fulfilling its dream of creating an integrated, modern, liberal state. Immigrants from Ontario and Europe were lured to the prairies, and its culture became decidedly "Canadian," the only question being whether or not "Canadian" would include French. By the late 1890s, that question too had been answered in the federal government's resolution of the Manitoba Schools Question. Ottawa was led, ironically, by a French-Canadian, Wilfrid Laurier, who accepted the principle of provincial rights and refused to disallow the Manitoba School Act of 1890 which had created an English, nonsectarian public school system for the province, despite the promise in the Riel-negotiated Manitoba Act of 1870 for a state-supported system, which included French-Canadian, Catholic schools.

The solution did not resolve the underlying federal/provincial conflict. Ever since, the federal government has continued to assert its position as the fundamental force behind the country's economic development, trade relations, immigration laws, cultural policy, foreign policy, and so forth. Provincial governments have fought not only for autonomy in areas defined as provincial in the BNA Act, but have also argued their right to resist federal policies which they believe interfere with their ability to serve the best interests of their constituents. After all, many provincial and regional leaders argue, who is best suited to determine those interests, the federal or provincial governments? But the liberal agenda has never been in doubt. The only debate has been about who controls its implementation.

By 1896, thus, the pattern of regional complaints and of provincial governments championing what they believe to be their rights was well established across the country. As the following examples illustrate, twentieth-century regional protest movements have consistently followed this pattern.

POST-WORLD WAR I

World War I, because of the federal government's heavy-handed and direct control over society and the economy, as illustrated in the War Measures Act and the rigging of federal election laws,[3] unleashed a torrent of regional dissatisfaction. This dissatisfaction was manifested most obviously in political movements across the country, whether Quebec's resistance to conscription, farmers' battles against tariffs and freight rates, or labour's struggle for collective bargaining rights.

One of these movements, the protest of farmers, began bearing fruit when the United Farmers of Ontario took power in 1919, followed by the United Farmers of Alberta in 1921, and the Progressives in Manitoba in 1922. These regional parties drew their support from an electorate concerned about the depopulation of rural areas and the threat of industrialization to their way of life. They argued that the federal system was weighted in favour of what they called the "eastern establishment." Eastern banks and railway companies, they argued, set rates for services which discriminated against farmers and favoured eastern industry and business. Furthermore, Ottawa (which they saw as eastern Canada's government) was responsible for the high cost to farmers of agricultural necessities such as machinery, implements, tools, and seeds because it used unnaturally high tariffs to protect eastern Canadian industry and business.

In 1919, ten MPs left government ranks to sit as members of a new party, the National Progressives. They managed to form the opposition in the federal election of 1921 when they sent 64 members to Parliament, 39 from the west, 24 from (mostly rural) Ontario, and one from the Maritimes. Committed to free-voting in Parliament, divided because of competing interests in Ontario and the Prairies, having virtually no representation in British Columbia, Quebec or the Maritimes, and watching the Liberals assimilate key elements of their platform, the Progressives lost support through the 1920s, and were essentially wiped out in the 1930 federal election.

But their complaints remained. After the Depression struck in 1929, the voices of western/prairie discontent resurfaced in the formation of two new political parties. The first was the Co-operative Commonwealth Federation (CCF) in 1933, which argued for a socialist state based on the nationalization of key resources, energy, banking, and industry, as well as for comprehensive social programs. The CCF, which became the NDP in 1961, achieved electoral success only in Saskatchewan, primarily because it abandoned a key element of its platform, namely, nationalization. The second regional party, Social Credit in Alberta, a populist party with an evangelical dislike of banks, big corporations, and the current financial order, achieved office in 1935, but because of the federal government's authority over fiscal and financial matters, was never able to make structural changes to Canada's financial system. It became instead a right-of-centre party, in the best tradition of pragmatic Canadian liberalism.

The Maritimes Rights Movement (MRM) did not have the same success as western protest movements. While economic misfortune because of the emerging national economy was also the basis of Maritime dissatisfaction, discontent did not spawn new parties. Instead, the MRM, born on the editorial pages of the Halifax *Herald* in July of 1922, stayed within the party-structure of the day and attempted to persuade the two traditional parties, the Liberals and the Conservatives, to adopt its platform of subsidies for poorer regions, more national trade through Maritime ports, and higher tariffs to protect Maritime economies — the opposite of the Progressive platform.[4] The MRM platform was the basis for H.W. Corning's Conservative Party's solid election victory in Nova Scotia in 1925 as well as for the near-Conservative sweep in the federal election of 1925. In 1926, King called a Royal Commission on Maritime complaints, but the movement faded away before a report was completed. Since then, movements and voters in the Maritimes have used the traditional party system to air their grievances. They have not created or embraced alternative parties.[5] But neither have their economic problems ended. The liberal dream of Canada has not been good to the Maritimes but they keep hoping that mega-projects like Hibernia Oil will turn around their fortunes.

QUEBEC

For more than one hundred years, from the mid-nineteenth to the mid-twentieth century, Quebec society was pervaded by a strong, conservative nationalism, nurtured on a myth of a defeated "people," abandoned by France in the conquest of 1760, denied their political and economic aspirations by the British in the rebellion of 1837-38, and surrounded, even besieged, ever since, by urbanizing, Protestant English who would never respect their agrarian, Roman Catholic way of life. From Louis-Hippolyte LaFontaine to Maurice Duplessis, this myth dominated French-Canadian provincial politics and underlay La-Fontaine's alliance with Robert Baldwin of Upper Canada in the 1840s, the acceptance of confederation (as a means to preserve French identity), the provincial rights assertions of Mercier, the resistance to fighting in the Boer War and both

World Wars, and the denial of suffrage to women in provincial elections until the late 1930s.

By the early twentieth century, everyday life began challenging the myth of an oppressed, rural, Catholic minority in America. By the time of Maurice Duplessis, Premier for most of the period from 1936-1959, Quebec society had undergone a radical transformation. Fewer people were living in the countryside; young men and women were flocking to urban areas in search of work. To accommodate this expanding French-Canadian working class, Duplessis welcomed foreign investment, especially American, to build an industrial society. But he persisted in the traditional myth of Quebec as rural and Catholic. The Catholic Church continued to control an education system based on a traditional, classical curriculum for the educated elite of French-Canadian society. Young people who wished to receive an education in technology, business, or other modern subjects had to go to anglophone institutions or leave the province. As a result, few received such training, and the control of commerce, industry, and business devolved to non-francophone Quebecers, especially investors, industrialists, and business people from the United States. The 1963 Royal Commission on Bilingualism and Biculturalism reported that French Canadians as group were on the lowest rungs of the income scale. Michel Brunet insisted that French Canadians had become "servants in their own home."

In the 1950s, serious intellectual movements began to challenge the myth. In June of 1950, Pierre Trudeau and Gerard Pelletier published the first edition of their new journal, *Cité Libre*. In it, they called for an end to the traditional myths, which, they said, no longer applied to modern, urban, industrial Quebec. They advocated the separation of church and state and called for the replacement of the Catholic-dominated education system by a secular, modern, public one, similar to those in other provinces. Instead of the old, French, collective nationalism, they promoted a liberal society which emphasized individual rights and freedoms. They urged Quebecers to accept and embrace modernity, and to take their place in Canadian society, in a new federalism, in which both levels of government would fully respect the rights which each had been given in the BNA Act.

In 1952, in contrast to the *Cité Libre* approach, Andre Laurendeau and Gerard Filion, among others, called for a "new nationalism." The *neo-nationalists,* as they were known, wished to reorient nationalism along urban, modern lines. They too accepted the need for a modern education system. They urged greater provincial government control over natural resources and industry so that the control over the economic and industrial development of Quebec would be in the hands of Quebecois.[6] But unlike *Cité Libre,* they believed that current constitutional arrangements were unsatisfactory, arguing instead for "special status" for Quebec within confederation.

Both perspectives reflected a growing desire for change in Quebec, and Quebecois responded by electing the Liberal Party, led by Jean Lesage, as their provincial government in 1960. In the so-called Quiet Revolution which followed, this government replaced the Church-controlled system with a public system geared to offering curricula appropriate to the modern world, one that would allow Quebec to create its own class of managers, scientists, industrialists, and businessmen. It nationalized most of the Hydro-electric system and set up various programs and incentives for Quebecois to become entrepreneurial and to take control over the economic life of the province.

But some Quebecois, strong voices from the left and weaker ones from the right, wanted more radical change, namely, an independent Quebec. One such leftist group, strongly influenced by the African decolonization movements of the 1950s and 1960s, created a journal, *Parti Pris,* which argued that nothing less than independence would end Quebec's colonial dependence on English Canada. They wanted to halt both the economic and cultural invasion of American popular culture, and, instead, create a Quebecois society which would serve the needs of the working people of Quebec. Around the same time, another group of separatist radicals, the *Front de libération du Québec,* began a systematic campaign of terror against English and federal institutions in Quebec, culminating in the October Crisis of 1970, when they kidnapped British Trade Commissioner James Cross and executed Quebec cabinet minister Pierre Laporte.

The separatist impulse received its defining moments when former Lesage cabinet minister, Rene Levesque, left the Liberal Party to create the Parti Quebecois in 1967 and one of the federalist founders of *Cité Libre,* Pierre Trudeau became the Prime Minister of Canada a year later. What followed was nothing less than a contest for the soul of Quebec. Committed to a traditional liberal philosophy and to keeping Canada intact, Trudeau immediately set out to patriate Canada's constitution and to negotiate a constitutional arrangement to satisfy all parts of the country. The first attempt at such an agreement, the Victoria Conference of 1971, failed when Quebec rejected the scheme. From that point, attempts to create a national agreement were unsuccessful. Trudeau oversaw the patriation of the constitution in 1982, but without the backing of Quebec. Subsequent efforts to gain Quebec support for the federal system, the Meech Lake and Charlottetown Accords, the product of his (fellow-Quebec) successor, the Progressive Conservative, Brian Mulroney, also failed.

Levesque fared little better than Trudeau. In 1976, he led his separatist Parti Quebecois to victory. But his 1980 referendum on separation (euphemistically called "sovereignty association") went down to defeat. Subsequent events — the further election of Parti Quebecois governments, the election of separatist Bloc Quebecois MPs to Ottawa, the referendum of 1995, and the inability of federal governments over the last twenty-six years to come up with acceptable constitutional arrangements with Quebec — have left the issue of Quebec separation from Canada unsettled.

There is an ironic twist to the issue, however. Both separatists and federalists in Quebec are committed to the same liberal, industrial, capitalist ideals which have driven this country since its inception and which have produced the kind of regional jealousies and tensions which are threatening Canada's future. The debate is essentially about power, about who gets to set the liberal agenda in Quebec. Quebec separatists believe that Quebecois control over a sovereign Quebec will redress alleged "injustices" perpetrated against them by federal control. The real problem is, and the topic of the debate should be, the liberal agenda itself.

RECENT WESTERN DISCONTENT

As has already been noted, western discontent, whether in dissatisfaction over payments and subsidies from Ottawa, the control of crown lands and resources (granted all provinces by 1930), French language issues, transportation policies, or the role of central Canadian banks and businesses, is as old as western Canadian membership in confederation. Western Canadian provinces, none of which has questioned the liberal vision, have seldom been pleased with the manner in which it has been implemented across the country.

In conjunction with the situation in Quebec, the latest round of western discontent may have more far-reaching consequences for the future of Canada than earlier ones. It has crystallized in the Reform Party, whose tough anti-government platform and hard-line attitude to Quebec may succeed in convincing Quebecers that the rest of Canada does not care if they leave confederation, something which Quebec separatists so far have been unable to persuade a majority of their people.

The discontent which spawned the Reform Party dates back to the early 1970s. In 1971, the people of oil-rich Alberta ended thirty-six years of Social Credit government by electing the Conservatives led by Peter Lougheed, who ran on an anti-Ottawa platform, asserting that federal policies were committed to maintaining the "Toronto-Montreal establishment" at the expense of the rest of the country. He argued that the citizens of Alberta received far too little from the oil which left their province and that, when the oil wells ran dry, Albertans would have little to replace their oil income if they had not established a wider industrial base.

Conflict between the two levels of government flared up in the oil crisis of 1973-74 when OPEC countries substantially increased the price of the oil they supplied to world markets. To protect industrial interests in central Canada, Ottawa responded to OPEC's rate increase by imposing price controls on the sale of domestic oil, at about half of the world price. Because these controls had a major impact on potential revenue

to Alberta coffers, Lougheed interpreted these controls as federal government protection of central Canadian interests, and
proceeded to circumvent them by doubling Alberta's rate of
royalties. Ottawa did not interfere. But Lougheed had seen the
enemy, and it was Ottawa. By the late 1970s, he was demanding
constitutional change in the form of a new division of power
between federal and provincial governments, particularly in
economic matters (in sharp contrast to Quebec which was ask-
ing for a new division of powers primarily in political and cultural areas).

The NDP government of neighbouring Saskatchewan, ob-
serving the Alberta action, also responded to federal price controls on oil by raising not only oil royalties, but also those on
potash. When the potash industry rebelled, the provincial government simply nationalized it, thus by-passing the issue of
royalties because the industry was now run by a crown corporation and, furthermore, avoiding federal taxes because crown
corporations were exempt from federal tax. They were not as
lucky with oil royalties. A challenge by the oil companies, supported by the federal government, resulted in a supreme court
decision which ruled that Saskatchewan's royalty scheme was
unconstitutional because it was an indirect tax. Curiously, the
oil companies never challenged the Alberta royalty scheme,
likely because the Alberta government was seen as free enterprise while that of Saskatchewan was NDP and, therefore, supposedly socialist.

The next move was Ottawa's. In October of 1980, Prime
Minister Trudeau announced the National Energy Program
(NEP) which would allow the federal government to use its
power to effect a minimum of 50% Canadian ownership of the
oil industry, and to achieve national self-sufficiency by 1990. To

do so, Ottawa would increase its tax on the industry, while reducing the allowable take of provincial governments.

Whatever the merits of this approach, Trudeau and the country paid dearly for the NEP, economically in the form of grants and tax exemptions given to the oil industry and politically in the rise of western discontent. In fact, a western separatist movement, the Western Canada Concept, managed to elect a provincial MLA in an Alberta by-election in 1982.

Although most western Canadians were not separatists, there was little doubt in the early 1980s that many of them were unhappy with Ottawa, reflected in the inability of the federal Liberal Party to elect members west of Manitoba in the 1980 election. In keeping with the neo-liberal, nostalgic milieu of the 1980s, there were many who hankered for the simpler, "good old days," when big government, big business, and big labour did not stand in the way of decent, Christian folks who wanted to work hard to make an honest living. Western anger over political, social, and economic issues was compounded by the failure of Ottawa to come to a satisfactory arrangement with Quebec. Quebecers were increasingly seen as "spoiled children" who would never be satisfied with anything that the rest of Canada would offer, no matter how generous. Instead, many westerners believed a hard-line approach was the only way to deal with Quebec.

Capitalizing on both the 1980s neo-liberal, anti-government sentiments and anti-Quebec feelings that were becoming ever stronger in western Canada, in 1987, political scientist and marketing consultant, Preston Manning, son of former Alberta Social Credit Premier Ernest Manning, created the Reform Party of Canada. It embraced a radical right-wing agenda, condemning Ottawa for wasting money, and calling for the end of the welfare state, "lax" immigration laws, and official bilingualism and multiculturalism. But it did not reject the liberal vision. Rather, it embraced such nineteenth-century, classic liberal ideals as laissez-faire economics and free trade, hoping that turning the clock back would magically undo what they saw as the damage of the Keynesian "welfare state" with its myriad restrictions and regulations on business and free enterprise.

In 1993, they elected over fifty MPs to Ottawa and came within one seat of becoming the official opposition. Their support was almost exclusively western Canadian; the party won only one seat east of Manitoba. The Parliament of the next three years was a strange place, as the only official parties were the governing Liberals, the anti-Canada, separatist Bloc Quebecois (as official opposition), and the anti-government, anti-Quebec Reform Party.

In the 1997 election, the Reform Party ran another anti-Quebec campaign, going so far as to state that Canadians should stop electing Quebecers to the position of Prime Minister and that Ottawa should deny "distinct society" status to Quebec. Their platform advocated dismantling the federal state by devolving departments and national standards on such things as health care to the provinces. This time they elected sixty MPs and became the official opposition. However, their popular support across the country declined, and all of their MPs were from the three western provinces. The separatist Bloc became the third party, but in Parliament there are two other official parties — the NDP and the Conservatives — whose perspectives on Canada are more traditional and akin to those of the Liberal Party than those of the two newer parties.

This study of regional conflict is by no means exhaustive but serves to point out that Canada, as it leaves the twentieth century, the century that Wilfrid Laurier boldly prophesied would be Canada's, has regional/provincial/federal conflicts serious enough to challenge its survival.

Perhaps, given its far-flung geography, a unified and cohesive Canada was an impossible dream. Still, the historical and current tensions between Canada and its regions were not inevitable, but the result of the attempt by the country's elites to create a liberal, industrial, technological empire in the northern half of North America. Liberalism was the means by which the confederation was formed and expanded, and liberalism dictated the relationship between its parts as well as the manner in which the country's central institutions attempted to integrate the regions, often contrary to the latter's desires or best interests. In the early 1920s, Arthur Meighen, even though he was attacking Mackenzie King's economic policies, described succinctly the nature of the Canadian state: "Protection on apples in British Columbia, Free Trade in the Prairie provinces and the rural parts of Ontario, Protection in the industrial centres in Ontario, Conscription in Quebec, and Humbug in the Maritime provinces." But few at the time, or since, have advocated abandoning the liberal dream. The battles among the various interests have been for the spoils of industrial, capitalist development and not for alternatives to it.

Jane Jacobs may be correct when she notes that national economies such as the one which Canada's elites have attempted to create are doomed to failure because they put unique regions, each with natural rhythms and cycles, into a centralized system whose priority is to meet the system's needs before those of its parts (see chapter 6 below). As the liberal elites lead Canadians to the global future, such national systems may be even more vulnerable to collapse. British Columbia's economy, for example, under the pressure of globalization, is currently being reoriented from the rest of Canada to Asia. Today's economic forces sometimes appear to be too powerful, and the country's elites' resolve too weak, for Canada to maintain the tenuous bonds which hold the country together.

As liberalism moves beyond nation states to trans-corporate globalism, we will likely witness ever stronger regionalism (perhaps even tribalism) as people fight to protect the well-being and interests of the places where they actually live, play, work, go to school, shop, and experience community.

ABOUT THOSE PLACES WHERE PEOPLE ACTUALLY LIVE

The liberal, capitalist forces undermining the unique identities and strengths of Canada's regions and communities are also undermining the structures of everyday life, as evidenced most clearly in the anonymous suburban environments in which the vast majority of Canadians now live. The development of suburbia has added yet one more element to the fight for regions to maintain their identities.

The suburban phenomenon, which has moved like a steamroller over the Canadian landscape, especially since World War II, promises "the good life" in the form of a lifestyle based on the liberal ideal of private property ownership and the "indefinite growth of the productive forces of economic life" (Elshtain, 1993). Ideologically, it ties nicely into the liberal, capitalist ideals of Canada's elites. The country's twentieth-century history shows that even as federal policies were integrating its economy, land-use and development policies were recasting Canada's physical landscape into suburban configurations increasingly similar to each other, and typical of regions and communities across North America.

The alteration to the country's landscape has been dramatic. As recently as 1900, the majority (60%) of Canadians lived in rural environments. Today's electronic mass communication technologies did not exist, identity and sense of place was local, and citizens' sense of being Canadian was defined predominantly by their local attachments. By the mid-1950s, this number had shrunk to 34% and is still declining. But the move from rural areas was not something about which many Canadians gave much thought; like "Topsy," suburbia "just growed." It was simply where most Canadians found themselves.

Having said that, however, the development of suburbia is rooted in British, colonial-Canadian land-use practices dating back to the late eighteenth and early nineteenth centuries. Unlike the seigneurial system of New France (and Quebec until 1854), where most people did not own land but worked on that owned by the nobility or large landowners, land in British colonies was treated as a commodity to be bought and sold for profit by individual landowners, to be used and settled as they saw fit. This fit John Locke's liberal ideal about the right of every individual to "life, liberty, and property." Influenced by contemporary notions of progress through rational order, colonial leaders, in disregard of topographical and natural features, imposed upon the landscape a grid system which divided the countryside into 640-acre sections of one square mile. The wilderness would be tamed; nature and the "wasteland" would be rid of undesirable features such as Natives and wild beasts. The process was similar to that of the English enclosure movement; the people removed in this instance were Native North Americans.

There were immediate problems. The sprawl created by this system of large, square chunks of land isolated neighbours from one another and worked against community life. Unlike in Quebec, where housing, businesses, trades, public places, and churches were integrated into community life and structures, and people could conduct most of their activities within a short distance from home, in English-speaking areas towns were spatially separate from where rural people lived. A well-developed road and transport system was essential if people wanted to shop, do business, school their children, go to church, or even visit neighbours.

After 1820, a communications revolution (one still not completed) began to overcome the limitations of this land-use system. Between 1820 and 1850, canal systems opened up the Great Lakes to Atlantic trade and allowed the use of recently invented steamships. After 1850, canals were followed by railways, encouraging movement of ever larger volumes of resources and goods, and ever greater numbers of people, from and into previously unconnected regions. Railways opened the prairies to European settlement after 1890, and Canada had its "bread basket." Canada's liberal elites' vision of a powerful, integrated, northern, industrial, capitalist economy, with each region making a particular contribution, could now be realized. But, as noted above, the seeds for regional animosities had also been planted.

After the turn of the century, nothing could match the automobile's capacity for the horizontal spread of human settlement. Those who could afford them were increasingly able to travel more freely over an ever larger number of lanes, roads, and highways.[7] The 1920s "roared" largely due to the enormous increase in the ownership of cars and the massive refitting of the landscape and infrastructure to accommodate them. Kenneth Norrie and Douglas Owram have noted that by the late 1920s, the automobile industry, when parts, gas, roads, and other related activities were factored in, was the largest industry in Canada. Farms near cities were subdivided to house people who could afford to move from cities to larger country dwellings. Homes were increasingly filled with the new gadgets, appliances, and widgets of the industrial age. Transportation allowed the spread of individualistic, consumer values into the countryside.

The bubble burst in 1929. But following the Depression of the 1930s and WW II, by the mid-1950s Canada's economy was again booming, fuelled by government policies which attracted millions of immigrants into the country and poured billions of dollars into infrastructure. As in the 1920s, the growth of transportation systems lay at the heart of the expanding good life. In the United States, the 1956 Highways Bill, promoted by such corporate lobbies as National City Lines (a partnership of General Motors, Standard Oil, and Firestone, formed to buy up and then shut down trolley and train systems), had a deceptively simple philosophy. Interstate highways would crisscross the countryside, by-passing cities so that automobiles, buses, and transport trucks could race across the country. On and off ramps would allow for easy access into and egress from cities. The military, in those tense years of the cold war, supported this system which, in the event of nuclear war, allegedly could move civilians, military equipment and personnel quickly and efficiently out of cities into the countryside. Canada's road-building since the early 1950s copied this United States' model.

Builders, auto-makers, and politicians across North America saw immense profit-making potential arising from these new roadways. They successfully persuaded millions of citizens to move from cities to new, huge instant subdivisions (the most famous of which was Levittown, New York) with cheap, affordable, mass-produced single-family houses, where they could have the "sense" of country living while working in the city. In suburbia, they could also realize the liberal dream of owning their own property (a fundamental "right"), and enjoying the consumption-oriented good life which it promised. New highways and freeways promised quick commutes to and from city jobs. Since the late 1950s, fully 70% of residential growth in Canada has been in suburbs.

But, alas, the dream was not everything that it promised. For one thing, despite the hope that suburban living would be an escape from ugly, polluted, and decaying central cities, a pastoral retreat, a taste of country life for all, many suburban landscapes retained little of the natural environment. Instead, residents found themselves living with polluted streams, denuded hillsides, scarce green-spaces, and chemically treated yards. Freeways connecting cities and suburbs, despite the promise of enhanced commuter mobility, quickly became jammed with vehicles, especially at rush-hour. Cities became congested with the automobiles of the very commuters who had fled them because of congestion.

Rather than restricting vehicle use, city politicians across Canada responded to congestion by building more car-parking facilities, a solution that usually made it worse. By the 1980s, fully one-third of the land of major Canadian cities was devoted to parking, and another twenty percent to roads, lanes, and alleys. City residents (often the poor who could not afford to leave) and businesses were saddled with ever-escalating tax bills as city governments attempted to continue to provide a wide array of services, many primarily for the benefit of the non-resident, non-tax-paying commuters.

Because cities are typically sited along rivers and transportation corridors and are often located on lands whose soils for growing food are of higher quality than elsewhere, the spread of the suburbia/freeway phenomenon on the outer edges of cities has also affected agriculture negatively. Such fertile land, generally flat and with easy access to water, is cheaper and simpler to build on than other terrains. According to an Environment Canada "Fact Sheet" (1986), from 1981-86, approximately 55,200 hectares of rural land were (sub)urbanized by 70 Canadian cities with populations over 25,000; land with prime capability to produce crops accounted for 50% of all land converted. To replace "the productive value of the prime agricultural land lost would mean developing and farming more than twice as much land in climatically marginal areas."

The land directly (sub)urbanized is accompanied by an "urban shadow," that is, land pulled out of agricultural production for speculation, often sold to non-farmers or held by "retired" farmers hoping eventually to develop it for residential, commercial, or industrial uses. Typically, for each acre consumed by urban development, a further two and a half acres are taken out of agricultural production in anticipation of urban expansion. As long as cities continue to move outward, there will be no end to the present double-bind of an ever-diminishing agricultural land-base and an ever-expanding population.

Industrial countries such as Canada solve this problem by importing ever-increasing amounts of less safe food from less reliable sources, delivered by transportation systems (truck, rail, or air) which, ironically, are largely responsible for the inappropriate use of local land (and loss of food-producing capability) in the first place. Regional self-reliance is negatively affected by this growing economic dependence on outside sources of basic necessities. Suburban development, thus, creates the very conditions which force regional economies into larger (provincial, national, and international) systems, but which, as regions attempt to protect their assets, also lead to the kind of confrontations between Ottawa and provincial/regional governments described above. In short, land-use patterns have a direct role in fostering the acrimony of regional tensions in Canada.

These are not the only costs. Suburbia makes genuine human interaction more difficult. The original grid, squared-section system of land distribution common across Canada has led to residential and commercial "strip developments" appearing haphazardly wherever developers can convince local officials to allow them. The "sprawl" pattern of development has few focal points or community centres; housing is isolated from shops, recreation facilities, entertainment, work, and schools. Instead of the more rounded and integrated life of traditional urban centres and older towns and small communities, suburbanites tend to have little sense of community and experience life as fragmented. Nearly every suburban function, whether picking up a six-pack or going to church, follows the example of the road, devouring space and time, creating ever greater amounts of frustration, and denying the possibility of easy meetings.

And family life suffers. After working couples or single parents spend most of their day commuting in automobiles and working, managing their household, and supervising their children's activities (often chauffeuring them from one pre-planned activity to another), they find a night in front of television easier than participating in community affairs, if they are even able to identify their community. Friends and relatives who could provide support and sustenance tend not to live nearby. As Betty Friedan pointed out about United States' suburbs in the 1950s, isolation and loneliness caused depression rates among suburban women to escalate. And as the taboo against divorce began to dissolve in the 1960s, divorce rates began to soar. The sad irony is that most people move to the suburbs hoping and expecting to enjoy easy, carefree lives.

The suburbanite's isolation leads to political apathy, at both local and higher levels; few understand how their communities work. If they are interested in knowing, the style of local government, with arcane zoning by-laws, municipal procedures, and political language, tends to frustrate and to discourage participation. Provincial and federal politicians have recognized this phenomenon, and, for the last several decades, have refocussed politics on media images, delivered primarily through the suburbanite's favourite medium, television. Suburbia discourages direct participation in democracy, especially at the local level. Voter turnouts are miserably poor in most city, town, and municipal elections.

In addition to environmental, social and political costs, suburbia, largely unplanned and uncoordinated, is prohibitively expensive in actual dollars. Typically, local governments borrow money to install infrastructure services such as sewer, water, garbage disposal, lighting, and sidewalks, the understanding being that developers who create new housing, factories, and stores will pass the costs of these services on to the purchasers of their developments. Repayment of loans made by local governments requires rapid development to avoid excessive interest payments for tax-payers. Therefore, suburban expansion often becomes a self-feeding monster, necessitating ever-faster rates of growth. When local governments run into financial difficulty in repaying their loans and in maintaining infrastructure, they are easily persuaded to allow the development of more land simply to pay off their debts. In New Jersey, for example, the *Globe and Mail* (1990) reported:

> The State planning commission has calculated that if all development were frozen now, the cost of carrying out needed capital infrastructure projects over the next twenty years will exceed available revenues by 1.66 times. Yet the rate of new development sprawl continues.

As senior governments in Canada download services to municipal governments and cut grant and/or aid programs, local government costs will continue to escalate.

The liberal values and practices to which Canadians have been committed since confederation, thus, have created a way of life which sacrifices regional and community uniqueness. This in turn gives most Canadians little choice but to live in the kind of suburban environments described above, and produces political apathy among residents by rendering local and regional politics virtually meaningless. The destination on this road is a homogenized future in which national and regional differences no longer matter because nothing is different and nothing is unique.

Therefore, rather than continually protesting about how "hard-done-by" they are in confederation, Canadians and their federal/provincial/regional leaders must re-examine the implications of continuing down the liberal, industrial path of development that has been the norm for all of Canada's history. They need to look more closely at how this commitment has shaped everyday life, particularly the contexts in which most people live out their daily lives in their regions and communities, the islands which constitute the Canadian archipelago. At stake is the possibility or impossibility of a unique, sovereign Canada.

NOTES

1 The regions into which Canada is divided fall into two categories. On the one hand, there are distinct geographical regions marked by variations in climate, topography, growing seasons, flora and fauna, and so forth. On the other, there is the constitutional division of the country into political units, that is, provinces and territories.

Historically, these categories have been blended, but, in popular and political circles, it is widely accepted that the country has six major regions: British Columbia, the North, the Prairies, Ontario, Quebec, and the Maritimes. While this division may be a distortion of both geography (northern Ontario and northern Quebec, e.g., being a natural geographical unit) and political history (compare politics in Saskatchewan and Alberta), it is useful in explaining how the parts of the country understand their place in the federal system. Regions outside of Ontario consistently have been unhappy with the federal arrangement, particularly with Ontario's perceived control of the federal agenda. The federal election of 1997 did nothing to allay this fear, as the Liberals swept almost all the seats in Ontario, that number allowing them to form the government.

2 In 1998, the federal government has rehabilitated Riel as a father of confederation. This only masks the real issue that Riel sought to address, namely the unfair and unjust treatment of the Métis and First Nations. Riel was not advocating the creation of the kind of Canada that Canadian leaders of the time were envisioning. In fact, his two rebellions were aimed precisely at opposing that model.

3 The Military Service Act, Military Voters Act, and Wartime Elections Act were passed in 1916 and 1917.

4 And a primary reason why regions across the country have been unable to work together in challenging federal dominance.

5 The 1998 election in Nova Scotia produced a Liberal minority government, with the NDP making an unprecedented breakthrough by electing the same number of MLAs as the Liberals and forming the opposition. It should be noted that the NDP is hardly a new alternative on the political scene. But it is significant that this is a departure from the Liberal/Conservative dominance which has characterized Nova Scotia for all of its provincial history.

6 Increasingly the word Quebecois is used instead of the traditional term, French-Canadian, an indication of a general, growing nationalism in Quebec.

7 It should be noted that the creation of this infrastructure was done largely at taxpayers' expense, benefiting primarily the automobile manufacturers and related industries as well as those who owned automobiles, but subsidized heavily by those who were unable to afford this new mode of transport. Public subsidy still enables the automobile industry to flourish and expand.

4

A KEY LIBERAL MYTH:
GROWTH AND DEVELOPMENT

> One hundred or 150 years ago our ancestors
> hoped that the railroad or the telegraph or the
> new highway would come close to where they were
> living, the sooner the better. In our time the news
> that a new highway or a new pipeline or a new
> development or a new shopping mall is coming
> close puts fear and loathing in our hearts.
> — John Lukacs, *The End of the Twentieth Century,*
> *and the End of the Modern Age*

Despite the economic and political problems created by the liberal dream — regional antagonisms among the country's many islands, costly suburban/sprawl development patterns, and political apathy — most Canadians and their leaders continue steadfastly to believe in its precepts, particularly its promise of a better future for everyone. Such acceptance does not arise from obstinacy or even stupidity but because liberalism, like all effective religions, philosophies, and ideologies, is sustained by powerful myths.

By myths we do not mean falsehoods or quaint stories, but deeply (often unconsciously) held beliefs and values that provide people with meaning and purpose, shape the way they live, guide their value-systems and world-views, and help them maintain faith in their society. Myths are the glue which holds cultures and societies together, which give people a reason for living. It is, therefore, not unusual for people to maintain faith in their myths despite destructive consequences of accompanying practices.

One of the dominant myths supporting the liberal ideal is that of "growth and development," which assumes that continual expansion, driven by modern technology, will bring humanity to ever higher levels of material and physical well-being. While the modern philosophical notion of growth and development dates back to the eighteenth-century Enlightenment, its current formulation and terminology became ingrained in the consciousness of North Americans and western Europeans only after World War II. In a 1949 speech, United States President Harry Truman used the word "developed" to describe the way of life of the world's industrialized countries. He pointed out that more than half of the world's people inhabited "underdeveloped" areas: "Their poverty is a threat to both them and to more prosperous areas." The "improvement" of these areas was both a moral obligation and a practical necessity; "development" would be the means. The world of his future would be a collection of homogeneous entities held together through economic interdependence, where the only significant differences among nations and peoples would be stages of "development" on the way to a prosperous future, that is, levels of acceptance and implementation of such elements as capital investment, industrialization, and modern technology. Cultural and nation-

106

al identities would become irrelevant.

Truman's pronouncement, a major step toward establishing the global, trans-national, corporate empires now dominating the world's economic scene, sent a quasi-religious message to whoever would listen that the liberal path of development was the inevitable unfolding of history towards a common destination — progress for the future. Most regions outside of the industrial west were classified as "underdeveloped" (the old colonial labels "savage" and "heathen" no longer being politically proper), while western nations and small pockets outside of the west were seen as "developed" and "modernized." "Development" would overcome the inequality between the west and the rest, the key means to advancement for the latter being the adoption of western educational, technological, industrial, military, medical, and economic models. It was, quite simply, a mid-twentieth-century version of Rudyard Kipling's "white man's burden."

So-called "under-" and "un-"developed peoples would know when they had become "modern" because, in true Enlightenment fashion, the "developed" world had created mathematical models defining progress on the road to development. Levels of development were statistically quantifiable. Per capita incomes, for example, showed not what people in "underdeveloped" countries actually had but what they lacked but could expect or hope to achieve in comparison with the accomplishments of people in countries like the United States. For those uncertain about how to reach this stage, the western world provided a coaching team: the IMF and the World Bank. The goal of development advocates such as Truman was nothing less than the globalization of the liberal, mechanistic and technological ideal. And woe to those who resisted or stood in the way of progress! If a technologically based, homogenized future was the *end,* growth and development would be the predominant *means.*

After the horrors of the Great Depression and World War II and the threatening atmosphere of the cold war, most Canadians, along with their North American and Western European contemporaries, readily embraced the growth and development myth. For Canada's people and leaders, this was not a major departure from the economic, political, and cultural ideals and practices which had dominated their country since the mid-nineteenth century. For Canadians, seeing themselves near the top of the development hierarchy only reinforced support for the myth.

And so, those of us born after World War II were thoroughly indoctrinated in the principles of the myth, being taught it by our parents, our teachers, our politicians, our economists, and our preachers. We grew up believing instinctively that Gross National Products, Gross Domestic Products, incomes, towns, cities, and countries *must expand,* even if the implications of this concept were beyond our comprehension. As children of the 1950s and 1960s, we were taught that Canada's history was the triumph of expansion, from the early heroic efforts of Cartier and de Champlain, who had come to an "empty" (Donald Creighton) and "barren" land, to the development of British colonies, and to the creation of an independent industrial, modern state.

As British Columbians, we watched proudly as Social Credit governments of the 1950s and 1960s built highways, ferry systems, and hydro-electric projects, while luring capital to exploit the province's minerals, fish, and forests. Instant modern towns sprang up around resource extraction and development sites, and the province's major urban/suburban areas expanded rapidly. Similar to patterns across Canada, the suburban juggernaut began to roll out around major urban centres throughout the province. Growth and development were recreating our physical world, and we were steadily becoming better off materially.

But it went further. The growth and development myth and corresponding practices which had become the "normal" state of our outer world also began to penetrate our inner worlds. From earliest youth, we were pushed not to accept ourselves as we were but to "make something" of ourselves: acquire higher education, aspire to good jobs, and strive for steadily increasing incomes, culminating in indexed pensions and well stocked RRSPs. Without growth and development, we were told, we would stagnate, whether on a personal or community level. Growth and development were irresistible, inevitable, and unstoppable forces to which we had to adapt and for which we had to plan. But we were taught that this was not a bad thing — such change represented "progress." By and large, most of us absorbed the message. After all, is that not how successful myths work?

And yet, as has already been noted, throughout the postwar era, there has been discontent and unhappiness throughout the country. Not only do regional leaders continually gripe about their peoples' sorry lot in confederation but everyday people are complaining about the breakdown of the country's social, economic, and cultural fabric. A serious gap appears to be opening up between the ideal of the myth of growth and development and the reality and practice of everyday life. By examining the history and practice of the growth and development myth in action in a particular region, and by exploring a number of serious problems associated with the myth, this chapter will point out major obstacles faced by residents in maintaining the unique regional identities which are crucial to the continuation of Canada as a sovereign state.

THE MYTH IN ACTION —
THE GREATER VICTORIA CASE

In the early 1990s, the Capital Regional District, the unelected regional government body overseeing British Columbia's Greater Victoria area, undertook a "visioning exercise" to ascertain residents' priorities in creating land-use and transportation policies to guide long-term planning. Much to the surprise of the researchers, rather than focussing primarily on land-use issues, a large majority of the respondents were predominantly concerned about "security," particularly the impact on their lives of (perceived) increasing levels of crime, prostitution, panhandling, homelessness, and other social ills. Their second item of concern was their fear that the region's natural environment was in a state of serious decline, and this was followed by worries about escalating population growth rates. Many of them clearly did not feel safe or comfortable at "home."

This dissatisfaction was also reflected in the voting patterns of the last two federal elections, when the largest block of support in the region went to the Reform Party of Canada. In the 1997 federal election, for example, many of the over forty percent of Greater Victoria residents who voted for Reform made it clear that they were displeased with how both federal and provincial governments were handling everyday matters such as crime and government services as well as national issues such as Quebec separatism. They wanted a crackdown on crime, lower taxes, and an end to Ottawa's pandering to "whining" from Quebec.

On the surface, such levels of dissatisfaction seem surprising, even frivolous. Major crime rates are actually declining, most of those who voted Reform are reasonably well off and live in relative comfort, and events in Quebec have little day-to-day relevance for most residents of Greater Victoria. The region also appears to have few of the social and environmental problems that plague many urban centres around the world. So why did participants in the survey respond the way that they did?

If we examine the cumulative impact of 150 years of serving first the interests of the British Empire and second of Canada, then evaluate the manner of local governance and human settlement patterns in the Greater Victoria region in terms of the growth and development myth, and finally point out the flaws of the myth, we begin to see that many of the region's residents, the vast majority of whom live in suburban environments, do not feel in control of their lives. This lack of control is a major reason for dissatisfaction and discontent.

A BRIEF HISTORY OF GROWTH AND DEVELOPMENT IN THE GREATER VICTORIA REGION

The history of the Greater Victoria area offers a particularly good illustration of the impact of the growth and development myth because, since the first Europeans settled here approximately 150 years ago, this myth, along with other liberal ideals, has been essentially unchallenged by other European or indigenous traditions in defining the values in which the residents believe, in shaping the region's demographic and settlement patterns, and in determining how its residents interact with each other and with the natural environment.

The first Europeans began living permanently in the region after 1843, when, following the closure of its operations on the Columbia River, the Hudson's Bay Company (HBC), established Fort Victoria as the new headquarters for its northwest coast department and for its Pacific operations. The move to Victoria represented retrenchment on the part of the HBC. Over the previous quarter century, as Richard Mackie has ably shown, the HBC, directed from London, with its west coast headquarters at Fort Vancouver on the Columbia River, had been successful in establishing a Pacific trade monopoly on the west coast of North America. Its land-based transport lines extended from southern Alaska through the interior of present-day British Columbia, Washington, and Oregon down to present day coastal California; its marine transport lines connected London, Fort Vancouver, and China, with Hawaii as a critical refueling and provisioning base. In addition to collecting and trading fur, by the 1830s, the company's activities included market farming, coal mining, timber harvesting, salmon processing, and trade with and provisioning of American and Russian ships. So successful was this Pacific trading system in extracting wealth from this area, that, according to James Gibson, it was responsible for approximately one-third of HBC profits between 1825 and 1846. The orientation of the first major European commercial activities on the west coast of what is now Canada was north/south and westward to the Pacific Ocean, directed from London.[1]

The move to Fort Victoria in 1843 was precipitated by declining returns on furs in the interior, the influx of white settlers into the Oregon area, and boundary negotiations with the United States, a process which the HBC believed would lead

Britain to concede a border north of the company's current headquarters on the mouth of the Columbia. Their fears were confirmed in the Oregon Treaty of 1846, which established the 49th parallel as the border between the United States and British possessions on the west coast, except for the southern tip of Vancouver Island.

The establishment of Fort Victoria also coincided with British imperial and global ambitions. In 1849, with the HBC as proprietor, Britain created the Colony of Vancouver Island to promote the settlement of surplus British population and to protect its strategic interests along the Pacific coast from further American and Russian expansion. British settlers, immigrants, businesses, and industries slowly followed, gradually creating a way of life and establishing cultural patterns similar to those of the places from which they had come.[2] By this point, liberal ideals of growth and development through capitalist, industrial, technological expansion were firmly in place in Britain. These would also be the ideals of the newcomers and would shape the transformation of the area from North American Native patterns of life and land-use to those of modern, liberal growth and development ideals, policies, and practices.

In the early 1850s, in order to facilitate this transformation, British colonial officials were authorized to sign fourteen treaties with the Natives of the Greater Victoria area and Vancouver Island, buying up Native territory but reserving land for their villages and promising them perpetual use of traditional hunting, gathering, and fishing areas. In the following decades, settlement and the implementation of modern land-use techniques made redundant the treaties' promises of Native rights to hunt, gather, and fish in traditional areas. By the 1860s, government and church leaders were urging Natives to abandon traditional styles of living and to adapt to the ways of the new-comers if they wished to survive. Ever since, they have had min-imal control over their lives and their original territory, and their pre-European values have had little impact in shaping and defining British Columbia's way of life. The Native ap-proach of adapting to the natural environment was replaced by one which sought to control and direct it along modern, liberal lines of expansion. For Europeans of the day, the area was an unspoiled, potential bonanza of untapped resources, a region ripe for western-style growth and development.

The 1858 gold rush into the interior of New Caledonia (on the mainland) accelerated this process of transforming the region to western standards of living. In that year, over 25,000 non-resident adventurers passed through Victoria on the way to the goldfields. Imports to the colony, which had totalled a mere $29,000 in 1857, reached $808,000 in July of 1858 alone. In the fall of that year, Britain organized its territory on the west coast of mainland North America into the colony of British Columbia.

By the mid-1860s, gold-panning had been replaced by capi-tal-intensive placer mining, managed by a wealthy, capitalist elite, most of which, particularly in the late-nineteenth century, would not take up residence in British Columbia. This pattern conformed to what had been established by the HBC and has remained true to the present. Outside capital and interests would dictate British Columbia's way of life and the manner of its expansion, placing the future of regions such as that of Greater Victoria in the hands and at the mercy of richer and more powerful capitalist structures and economies.

The governments created in the two colonies reflected cur-rent liberal practice in Britain. Governors were appointed by the crown, and gradually elective legislative assemblies, with limited, (white) male suffrage based on property ownership, were established. Natives were not given the vote. The same system was carried over when the two colonies merged into the colony of British Columbia in 1866. At that time, as Keith Ralston, Robert McDonald, and J.M.S. Careless have shown, Victoria was British Columbia's economic centre and, as in the days of the HBC empire, its business and commercial interests were oriented to the Pacific, now connected to and dominated by British and San Francisco financial interests.

Three shifts in international and continental forces in the mid-nineteenth century would redefine Victoria's place in the scheme of things. The first was Britain's growing desire to divest itself of the administrative and military costs of colonies with dominant white populations. The second, a product of the first, was the 1867 union of four British colonies, north of the United States, into the self-governing colony known as the Dominion of Canada. Its leaders recognized the potential resource wealth of British Columbia for central Canadian industrial development (see chapter 2). The third was the United States' notion of "manifest destiny," with many prominent Americans seeing the future of North America as being under the "stars and stripes." Canada and Britain teamed up to block the plans of the United States for expansion. Overcoming local resistance, they offered to cancel British Columbia's large colonial debt (the result of a decline in gold rush revenue) and promised it a transcontinental railway link to the rest of Canada within ten years. British Columbia's leaders were persuaded, and their colony joined confederation as Canada's sixth province in July of 1871. The structure and form of the new province's government were defined by the British North America

Act (see chapter 3). Natives were placed under the control of Ottawa.

Because of the natural barrier of the Rocky Mountains and the lack of communications systems across the northern half of North America, Victoria's economy, like that of British Columbia as a whole, initially changed little after confederation because it had little orientation to regions east of the Rockies, at least not until the completion of the CPR in 1885. In the 1880s, not because of its place within Canada's economic system but because of its continuing Pacific links, its economy actually boomed, its capitalist classes directing lucrative industries in sealing, salmon canning, carriage making, brewing, and tourism. By 1890, it was estimated that Victoria's wealth was three times that of Nanaimo, Vancouver, and New Westminster combined. The confidence of the 1890s was reflected in the development of many of Victoria's older, wealthier neighbourhoods, the establishment of a public streetcar system, and the construction of the Parliament Buildings (opened in 1898) at a cost of more than half the annual provincial budget.

By 1900, the city had dropped from fifth to twentieth among large Canadian cities in per capita manufacturing output, even while the economy of British Columbia as a whole increased sharply. There were two major reasons for this change. The first was the 1886 completion of the transcontinental railway with its western terminus in the newly incorporated city of Vancouver rather than at Victoria (along the Bute Inlet route as originally promised), which shifted the focus of British Columbia's economy to the mainland. Vancouver became the centre from which new and larger, heavily capitalized (predominantly by non-locals) companies would operate, whether to underwrite consolidation movements in the lumber and salmon industries or to direct the discovery of enormous mineral deposits in the Kootenays.

A second reason for the decline of Victoria's role as a strategic trading and manufacturing centre was the federal government's National Policy which, because it placed high tariffs on imports, reoriented British Columbia's economy away from the Pacific, eastward, to the rest of Canada. Victoria was isolated by federal policy and economic change, a result of the central Canadian elites imposing their vision upon the rest of the country.

As a result of this isolation, for the first half of the twentieth century, life in the Victoria area changed little. In the "roaring twenties," the city's population actually declined, the 1931 census figure of 39,000 being less than that of 1911. Had Victoria not been the capital of British Columbia, the economic and population declines would likely have been greater. The tourism industry expanded, from 200,000 tourists in 1923 to 360,000 in 1927. By the late 1930s, the number of jobs in the three levels of government, particularly provincial, exceeded those from any other category. Secondary industry remained relatively undeveloped.

The 1950s saw a departure from these decades-long economic and population patterns and the end of isolation. The country's optimistic, post-war growth and development "bug" (see chapters 2 and 3) hit the city, and the population of the Greater Victoria region increased quickly, from a little over 100,000 people in 1951 to 175,000 by 1966, and 325,000 by 1996 — a 225% increase in forty-five years. Expansion was largely fuelled by outsiders' perceptions of the area's merits, particularly as illustrated in a continued increase in the number of tourists and an influx of pensioned retirees. The government of British Columbia responded to these outside pressures by dramatically expanding the ferry service between the mainland of British Columbia and Vancouver Island after 1960, and by establishing the University of Victoria in 1963. Most of the new residents, following patterns similar to those of other North American cities of the time, settled in the city's suburbs rather than in its urban core. The City of Victoria contained 59% of the Metro population in 1941; by 1971, it had only 28%. The sprawling, suburban municipality of Saanich has had a larger population than Victoria since 1966; by 1996, it had twice the number of people. Also by 1971, tourism-related employment was higher than that of any other sector, followed by public administration and government, particularly federal and provincial.

As this brief overview clearly illustrates, while specifics may differ, the story of Victoria resembles that of regions across Canada. For the past 150 years, control over its way of life and the cycles of its economy has not been in the hands of its residents but has been dominated by large, more powerful, outside forces committed to the liberal myth of growth and development, whether British or Canadian. This domination has accorded with the wishes of the country's elites who, as noted in chapter 2, have been striving since the mid-nineteenth century to build a progressive, Canadian, liberal state north of the United States. Because residents have such little control over their destiny, it is small wonder that many of them are dissatisfied and cynical about those who govern them, and are sympathetic, even supportive, of regionally based protest movements.

But the dissatisfaction runs deeper than mere anger at powerful, outside forces serving the interests of the country's elites. As the Capital Regional District's "visioning" exercise illustrat-

ed, many people are insecure about their homes, their neighbourhoods, and their communities. In short, the liberal myth
of growth and development not only explains the macro-eco-
nomic systems of Canada and the creation of regional discontent but is also integral to understanding the forces and government structures which shape the communities in which
people live their everyday lives and about which they are dissatisfied.

LOCAL EXAMPLES

To understand the nature of this dissatisfaction, it is helpful
to look at the sub-regions of the Greater Victoria region, the
communities in which people actually live, eat, work, play, and
sleep. It is there that the shape and the meaning of the liberal
dream and of its supporting myth of growth and development
show up most obviously, particularly in the manner in which
Europeans have altered the landscape and geography over the
last 150 years.

Like those across Canada, the region's land-use patterns
were not the product of any grand design or master plan. Local
government officials, often acting as agents for special interest
groups such as business elites, developers, and/or land-specu-
lators, and obediently following the precepts of the growth and
development myth, allowed the landscape to be remade according to the liberal dream of a private estate for every family,
and, particularly after World War II, a domain complete with
automobiles and the consumer trappings deemed necessary
for individual happiness. Politicians and their electorates
seldom questioned their allegiance to the myth (if they even
understood it) and rarely gave thought to long-term social,

environmental, and economic consequences of local land-use approaches.

The case of Central Saanich, the community in which I live, a small, Greater Victoria suburban/rural municipality of about twenty square miles and 16,000 people, on the Saanich Peninsula, fifteen kilometers outside of the city of Victoria, serves as a useful illustration of the manner in which growth and development not only dominates local politics but appears to be an unstoppable juggernaut. Farmland and second-growth hillsides dominate its landscape. Forty-two percent of its land-base is protected from urban/suburban development by a provincially controlled Agricultural Land Reserve (ALR). Residential and commercial development has taken place predominantly in three compact residential pockets, two with small-town villages. These residential areas are looking increasingly like typical suburban areas elsewhere in the country, and pressure is growing for the spread of development between these pockets — that is, to "sprawl" them into one continuous residential, suburban area. Central Saanich's residents are relatively affluent and professional, the large majority working in service industries, education, or the various levels of government. In short, despite its agricultural look and rural focus, it is primarily a bedroom community for Victoria.

Provincial law requires all municipalities in British Columbia to adopt an Official Community Plan (OCP) to guide land-use planning. Central Saanich's first OCPs, in 1979 and 1984, were committed to the preservation of the small-town, rural character of the municipality, to the protection of its agricultural land, and to a slow rate of growth, with an ultimate population level of approximately 15,000 people, to be reached early in the twenty-first century. Rapid growth in the 1980s — the result of an expanding economy, the region's favourable climate, and the desirability of living in small rural-looking towns a short distance from an urban centre — eroded the municipality's supply of easily developable land. Land speculators and developers began lobbying the local council with applications to rezone and develop agricultural land (flat and easily developable) protected from development by the ALR.

In 1989, in response to these requests, the municipal council presented the public with a number of options for revisions to its OCP. These ranged from the current upper population level of 15,000+ people to an option calling for the removal of large amounts of land from the ALR for housing, commercial development, and golf courses — virtually doubling the population ceiling to 29,730. In questionnaires administered by the council, 63% of respondents wished to maintain the present upper population level or even lower it. An even larger percentage opposed the use of ALR land for non-agricultural development or for golf courses.

In the summer of 1990, claiming to have produced a compromise between land speculators and residents, the council adopted a new OCP which called for a maximum population capacity of over 19,000 and the use of agricultural land for golf courses. Despite what residents had clearly told them, the council also committed the municipality to speeding up and facilitating the process for the development of areas currently not slated for development.

In the 1990 municipal election, the majority of residents who voted (there is typically a 35-45% voter turnout in Central Saanich municipal elections) elected a council opposed to the pro-development policies of the previous three years. It amended the new OCP to reflect a vision corresponding to what a majority of respondents had indicated in the questionnaires of 1989, and it implemented measures to slow the rate of population growth. At the next election, 1993, the land speculation/ development industry poured money into a slick campaign which led to the election of a development-oriented council. For this industry, the stakes were high; easily developable land near an urban centre can realize huge profits. For three years, over constant objections from the public, this council supported virtually every development proposal which crossed its table. In the 1996 election, pro-development candidates were routed. The new council was committed to as little development as possible, resulting in an almost immediate creation of a counter-force, ready to wage the next election.

The case of Central Saanich illustrates the polarized politics and the pressures facing hundreds of small communities across the country, especially those near large urban centres with easily developable agricultural land.[3] Local government politics are invariably dominated by growth and development issues, pitting those desiring expansion and change against those who wish to see as little alteration to their communities and lives as possible. In the present system of local government, there are no real solutions to this fundamental tension. The reason is structural: a handful of elected officials is given total power to manage a community's affairs for three years and to change (or not change) land-use and zoning patterns without being *required* to respect the needs and wishes of residents. Communities can be changed quickly and radically in ways that the residents do not approve. In short, residents are powerless to stop their elected officials, except in elections. As a result, most people believe that "it really doesn't matter" whom they support (most are convinced that development-oriented special interest groups dominate local politics), and voter turnout in local elections — for offices governing the places closest to home — is the lowest of the three levels of government in Canada.

At the regional level, residents are even more powerless. Regional governments in British Columbia are predominantly appointed rather than elected. Hence, they have even less accountability to residents than local governments whose leaders must, at least, be elected. Residents often perceive regional governments as faceless bureaucracies, acting as agents for the development industry.

The regional government of the Greater Victoria area, the Capital Regional District (CRD), illustrates this point clearly. In April 1990, it published a report entitled, "Regional Growth Review — Victoria Metropolitan Area, 1989-2011," which projected a population growth rate for the region for that period of 18.8%, or approximately 52,000 people, and between 20,000 and 25,000 new dwellings. It defined its purpose as follows: "to determine if the current planning policies of the municipalities and electoral areas allow for sufficient land to be developed to accommodate this projected growth" (not if such accommodation should occur!). Because the report noted the region's governments were not freeing up enough land for development to meet the CRD's targets, each area and municipality in the CRD was *instructed* to "consider whether their Official Community Plan identifies sufficient development potential to accommodate these projections." A follow-up report argued that local governments' OCPs and "sensitive natural environments" (which it defined as land that was "environmentally constrained") should not be a barrier to development. Both reports, driven by the development industry's demands for more developable land, assumed the continuation of the suburban-sprawl land-use and housing patterns of the last three decades. Neither report had included any environmental, economic, or social impact analyses to support the land-use recommendations. Nor had the reports made any attempt to solicit public input or to offer alternatives to current land-use patterns or to the ideal of growth and development.

The CRD is presently undertaking a provincially mandated regional plan for the Greater Victoria Area, to be completed some time in 1999. Public response has been minimal. Even those residents who pay attention to political and land-use matters, who dutifully attend meetings, and who fill out questionnaires doubt that a regional plan will have a significant impact on the issues which concern them most — the perceived levels of rising crime and the continued erosion of the natural environment. They believe (correctly) that the CRD board and its bureaucrats assume the continuing spread of suburban, single-family-housing and commercial sprawl. In April 1998, a major public meeting, organized by the CRD to solicit residents' response to a draft proposal for a regional plan, was structured to allow only 40 members of the general public (out of a population of over 330,000) to speak. There is a large gap between resident input and the manner in which the growth and development ideal is implemented.

Moreover, British Columbia's provincial government has still less respect for citizens' concerns than local and regional governments. Because it creates and regulates local and regional governments, the province has no obligation (other than moral) to respect local OCPSs, zoning by-laws, or any measures passed by local or regional governments. In transportation planning, for example, its Ministry of Transportation and

Highways (MOTH), in true nineteenth-century Canadian Pacific Railway style, has a history of running roughshod over local communities' objections to plans to create new provincial transport systems. Because of the provincial government's legislative authority, citizens and small communities possess no avenues of redress with the government if it creates laws and sets policies which involve irresponsible land-use planning, spoliation of the natural environment, or social and economic recklessness. In short, there are no laws to rein in the law-makers, except the ones they create themselves.

A current example of both the provincial government's commitment to growth and development and its disregard for citizens, communities, and regions, is MOTH's mega-project recasting Vancouver Island's main transportation corridor into a typical North American, high-speed expressway/freeway system.[4] For the Greater Victoria area, this project has radical implications, because the City of Victoria, the province's capital and southernmost point of Vancouver Island, is the major destination for traffic from the rest (northern parts) of Vancouver Island via the Island Highway as well as from mainland British Columbia via the Swartz Bay ferry terminal and the four-lane Pat Bay Highway. There are daily rush-hour traffic backups into the city on the Island Highway from up-Island commuters, while traffic on the Pat Bay Highway, which runs north/south along the narrow, mixed suburban/rural Saanich Peninsula from Swartz Bay, flows relatively smoothly all day. But there is increasing congestion on Victoria's streets, its arteries clogged by growing volumes of automobile traffic, despite the creation of ever more parking space. A regional bus system is an alternative to the automobile, but it is mostly slow, inconvenient, and indirect.

The reconstruction of the Island's transportation system was initiated in 1988, at an estimated cost of well over a billion dollars, the costliest mega-project in British Columbia's history. Because OCPs had been ignored and local residents had not been consulted, MOTH faced immediate opposition to its plans. Island-wide coalitions, with dozens of groups and thousands of members quickly formed, requesting a moratorium on freeway planning until MOTH had released background studies about traffic flows and projections, designs, environmental/ social impacts, alternative modes of transport, etc. so that residents could understand the rationale for the project and the impacts upon their lives.

Critics quickly learned that there were no such studies. Moreover, as the critics probed ever more deeply into the government's planning processes and watched as the government broke the Island Highway mega-project down into scores of "small projects," it became apparent that the government had no overall plan, that the expanded highway was being designed and built piece-meal. This approach had the advantage of exempting the government from its own legislation requiring environmental impact studies on mega-projects. So much for governments respecting citizens, communities, or even their own laws.

PROBLEMS WITH THE GROWTH AND DEVELOPMENT MYTH

The above examples illustrate how the growth and development myth runs roughshod over most obstacles that stand in the way of its view of "progress," including democratic participation by citizens. But growth and development is about much more than residents' negative feelings or a lack of democracy. As historian John Lukacs has noted, it underlies a particular way of thinking about and of relating to the world: "Most of us know how often development amounts not to opening but to closing, how it means the eager spreading of cement and the indifferent razing of the land. We know how often construction means destruction — not only of trees and meadows but of certain ways of life." Father Raimon Panikkar echoes this sentiment and has pointed out that, while development is often identified with "progress, well-being, and happiness," it enters cultures by "bulldozers, tractors, and all the rest. . . ." Once people accept this way of "thinking" and "doing," they end up "having to adapt to [the machines'] ways of thinking," creating a dependence on a style of technology which effectively and essentially eliminates alternative methods of living with nature. Instead of happiness and the good life, he concludes, people find enslavement to the world of the machine and all it represents.

The failure to deliver on its promise of the "good life" may also result from the fact that liberal growth and development seems to have no clear sense of purpose or ultimate destination, other than some open-ended, vaguely-defined, technologically based, homogenized future or its self-perpetuation.[5] In fact, for many proponents, this lack of purpose is seen as a good thing, because growth and development, similar to how neo-liberals view today's market economy, should simply be allowed to happen with minimal interference, the means being assumed as "natural" and "right." Those who disagree are not only old-fashioned and reactionary, but are fighting historical inevitability.

This assumption of "natural" and "right," however, is inherently dangerous because it implies that no one has to take responsibility for consequences, whether economic, political, social, or environmental. For example, while the ideal of growth and development has ended the hardship of subsistence living for many, it has also ruined self-reliance, that is, local control over lands, trees, and waters. Instead, it has made people dependent upon outside economic forces over which they have no control for such basic necessities as food, clothing, shelter, and transportation. For many Canadians, this lack of self-sufficiency, in combination with cuts to social services of the last decade or so, has potentially serious consequences should a disaster similar to the Depression of the 1930s recur. The assumption, therefore, that modern growth and development patterns and the resulting lack of self-reliance are both "natural" and "right" is unwise and negligent. Canadians need to begin to accept responsibility for the consequences of both their collective and personal actions.

In recent years, in partial response to these concerns, there have been growing numbers of experts, politicians, business people, and ordinary citizens who argue that the problems of growth and development can be overcome by adopting good methods of growth and development, reflected in terms such as "managing growth" or "sustainable development."[6] Advocates of such terms believe that humans can maintain continuous growth and development while still safeguarding the natural environment. The term "sustainable development," however, is an oxymoron: sustainable development is still development, and the kind of breaking of natural rhythms which accompanies the *modern* practice of growth and development invariably means the end of sustainability. Ursula Franklin has persuasively argued that limitless growth and development, including that of human population, is not only unsustainable, but mathematically impossible. The earth lacks the resources and capacity to feed and supply an infinitely expanding number of people.

The popularity of the concept of "sustainable development" is likely based on the fact that the country's elites (elected government officials and their bureaucrats, business and corporate leaders, bankers, and other leading agents of liberalism) can pay lip-service to something that the public is increasingly demanding of them and then go about business as usual. They hire experts and public relations wizards to convince Canadians that they are managing Canada's resources sustainably, are concerned about the health of the natural environment, and are responsibly balancing environmental and economic needs. The rhetoric is designed to make Canadians feel better about the management of their communities and believe that negative and destructive consequences of growth and development are largely issues of the past. But since the term has become fashionable, there has been little appreciable difference in how regions like that of Greater Victoria have continued to be altered. In short, there has been no change to the sprawling, car-oriented, suburban, residential/commercial land-use patterns of the last fifty years.

The term "sustainable development" is also problematic from a philosophical perspective, particularly in its frequent advocacy of the "systems" approach, which, in true Enlightenment fashion, sees the world as a large managerial system bound by abstract equations. It treats people, food, and resources as manipulable components of that system, which, when properly understood and programmed into computer formulae and models, can produce appropriate planning techniques. But nature, people, and resources are not reducible to easy, universal equations, the rhetoric of engineers and managers, the language of control. Nor should problems with the natural environment be treated simply as technical and managerial problems which will disappear with appropriate technical and managerial solutions.

Those who raise questions seriously challenging these current approaches to dealing with the natural environment find few friends in government, whether at national, state/provincial, city, county/regional, or municipal levels. At the local, regional, and provincial government levels, politicians and their supporting casts of bureaucrats and consultants typically view themselves as active proponents, even agents, of growth and development, "sustainable" or otherwise.

This relationship of government to the forces of growth and development poses serious challenges to the very nature of government, particularly concerning its responsibility to citizens. As long as Canadians remain committed to the expansion and development of their urban/suburban, technological, industrial way of life, their country will require ever more extensive and costly infrastructure to service it. If its federal and provincial governments are to do the task for which they were created, namely, protecting citizens' rights and freedoms by ensuring justice, fairness, environmental safety, social safety nets, and so forth, they will have to play a key role in directing the creation and maintenance of such infrastructure. Furthermore, as the world which liberalism builds becomes increasingly complex, if governments are to serve the public interest, they will have little choice but to adopt a larger regulatory role.[7] Growth and development, therefore, as it creates an ever more complex world, necessitates ever more bureaucratic governmental systems which require ever larger amounts of spending, taxes, and revenue.

Contemporary governments face serious conflicts of interest in dealing with this duality of promoting growth and development, while at the same time protecting the interests of public good and the rights of individuals. An excellent example is British Columbia's forest policy. The vast majority of the province's harvestable forest areas are provincial crown lands leased to private companies. The more assiduously trees are cut, the greater the revenue flowing to the crown and the more money they have available for regulatory agencies or for social services such as education and health care. However, because crown lands belong to all British Columbians, the provincial government also occupies a fiduciary and stewardship position with respect to these lands. Up to this point, the forest companies' need for profit and the government's need for revenue have been taking precedence over the public good, that is, the need to protect the forests or benefit local communities.[8] One result of this approach is that the forest industry in British Columbia is now in deep trouble — fewer good trees, loss of jobs due to automation, and declining revenue for the provincial government. The public good and the natural environment appear to be suffering because of growth and development.

The choice Canadians face is straightforward. If they want to continue on the growth and development path, as well as to maintain environmental, social, economic, health and other such safeguards for their citizens, the size of governments will of necessity continue to expand. However, if the current neo-liberal trend of cutting legitimate government functions and/ or putting them in private hands continues, it will be those who most need the protection and assistance which the modern state currently (and correctly, albeit imperfectly) offers — those unable to work, the sick, the poor, the elderly, the children, etc.

— who will bear the brunt of this near-sighted philosophy. And the natural environment, which cannot speak for itself, but relies on humanity's stewardship, will suffer even more if Canadians maintain their commitment to the myth of growth and development while at the same time continuing current, neo-liberal-driven government downsizing and deregulation trends. Even with the present regulatory framework, nature has enough of a problem. It is immoral to neglect the social and environmental costs of the liberal growth and development machine as neo-liberalism is inclined to do.

In the current political environment, there seems to be no way out of this dilemma. Aspirants to political office who challenge the premises of the growth and development model are doomed to short careers, if they can even launch them. In most elections, successful candidates are those who argue that growth expands the tax base and allows more services. Indeed, most candidates and politicians trip over each other to attract investment, pitting party against party, city against city, and region against region, and competing for roads, museums, convention centres, company headquarters (or subsidiaries), athletic teams, athletic events, union halls, and mega-stores. No wonder people believe, as Grant argued many years ago, that politicians seem more eager to please the elites than ordinary people.

This narrow- and single-minded focus of politicians is also largely responsible for citizen antipathy for politics. Most of them believe that governments, from federal to provincial to local, do not represent "the people," but rather are their opponents.[9] Alan Cairns has noted that on the federal and provincial scenes in Canada, citizens are "little more than spectators, mobilized by competing elites at three-to-five year intervals for electoral purposes, and then returned to their accustomed role as objects of government policy." For the well-being of the country's so-called democracy, Canadians cannot afford to maintain this relationship between people and governments. Only healthy democracies, at all levels, can begin to resist the lure of globalization and put power into the hands of communities.

Like that of other regions across Canada, the history of Greater Victoria and the case-studies of Central Saanich, the Capital Regional District, and British Columbia's Ministry of Transportation and Highways clearly illustrate how deeply the growth and development myth has permeated the everyday lives of Canadians and the systems that govern them. It has also shown that ordinary people have major battles on their hands when they attempt to challenge current government practices in order to gain a greater degree of control over the shape and future of their regions and communities and to design them to meet human and nature's ends rather than those of the liberal way of life and of the elites promoting it.

Unless Canadians take up this challenge, however, Canada will simply fade away, with little fanfare, blending into what George Grant called the "homogeneous future" of the liberal dream, an indistinguishable global, consumer reality. But to take it up, Canadians will need to understand more fully the nature of the liberal value-system underlying the growth and development myth and the manner in which it has shaped regions such as that of Greater Victoria.

To that we shall now turn.

NOTES

1 Both the HBC and its predecessor, the North West Company, had attempted to establish east-west supply lines from the Hudson's Bay and Montreal. These proved too costly. The interior posts established after 1800 in central and northern British Columbia became part of a complicated brigade system which ended at Fort Vancouver on the Columbia River. Both Mackie and Archer describe a trade system, west of the Rockies, with a north/south orientation, a model which runs counter to Harold Innis's commonly accepted east/west explanation of Canadian development. While Innis is correct in his contention that the fur trade opened the way for settlement in British Columbia and that the inspiration for western Canadian exploration and trade came from the east, British Columbia's trade and settlement patterns were north-south, not east-west, at least until the completion of the CPR in 1886.

2 It is worth noting that the European segment of British Columbia's history begins much later than that of the rest of Canada — the early settlements in Quebec predated those of the west coast by more than two hundred years. For British Columbians, there is little connection to or shared memory of the geographical, material, and mental landscapes of central and eastern Canada.

3 One solution, adopted by the provincial government of Ontario, is to amalgamate small communities such as Central Saanich with other local governments to create super municipalities. This does not solve the problem of sprawl or eliminate conflict between development and anti-development groups. It merely removes citizens' easy access to government.

4 Study after study makes the irrefutable case that the building of freeway/super highway systems is the major catalyst for suburban sprawl. See also the previous chapter's discussion of suburbs. And, for British Columbia, it has made little difference whether the government has been Social Credit or NDP.

5 Note, for example, that the term "Gross National Product," the measure of total income that flows into an economy, is detached from any real value other than quantification. As Jose Lutzenberger has pointed

out: "When a plane crashes, say a 747 jumbo-jet, that moves more than a million dollars, the amount the airline receives from the insurance company. When the airline buys a new plane, the GNP grows by the same amount again. And if there are survivors, all the medical and health care costs will also increase the GNP, as will the bills of the undertakers who bury the dead. So the more accidents and calamities we have, the better."

6 Some advocates of this idea support preserving large blocks of the natural environment in their allegedly "natural" state, in the name of protecting biodiversity, underscoring the fact that late twentieth-century homo-sapiens cannot be trusted to live in and with nature but must set it aside to protect its integrity.

7 For example, the complex ethical questions raised by computer/internet and genetic technologies.

8 The provincial government recently rejected a community-based application for a woodlot license tenure on Malcolm Island (*Monday Magazine,* Dec. 4-10, 1997), preferring to keep the tenure tied to big forest companies and union jobs. Would it not make some sense to begin moving stewardship of the forests to the communities in and around the forests?

9 Many people would agree with at least two-thirds of Oscar Wilde's assertion that "High hopes were once formed of democracy, but democracy simply means the bludgeoning of the people, by the people, for the people."

5

THE HEART
OF THE MATTER

Turning and turning in the widening gyre
The falcon cannot hear the falconer;
Things fall apart; the centre cannot hold;
Mere anarchy is loosed upon the world,
The blood-dimmed tide is loosed, and everywhere
The ceremony of innocence is drowned;
The best lack all conviction, while the worst
Are full of passionate intensity.

— William Butler Yeats, "The Second Coming"

George Grant's major contribution to the study of Canadian society was his perception that Canada's survival as a unique, sovereign country was seriously jeopardized by the ubiquitous belief of its political, economic, and intellectual elites that the only value system that mattered to the modern age was that of liberalism, whose political and economic practices he claimed were homogenizing nations and cultures around the globe. He called this drive to global homogenization the "modern project," and argued that "modern technology" was its primary instrument in displacing and even destroying the values which had, until modern times, shaped western civilization since its Judaeo-Christian/Greek origins. Adherence to the modern project would make values such as patriotism and national pride anachronistic. Canada would begin to matter less and less.

By "modern technology" he did not mean technology in the broad, general sense of the word. He recognized that technology is as old as human existence; human beings have always been "making" and "doing." Rather, his concern about the potentially destructive impacts of modern technology was derived from his insight that technology was never neutral but always contained an embedded value-system and was always a product of a world-view, of the vision its creators had of the world.

Grant argued that the value system and world-view which underlay modern technology was that of the seventeenth- and eighteenth-century Enlightenment, which (as noted in chapter 1) had suggested an alternative to religiously based ideas of truth founded on revelation and divine authority. It had argued for the truth, accuracy, and reliability of knowledge derived from observation, deduction, and mathematical calculation. "Objective" truth, derived from nature, measurable, quantifiable, and/ or logically provable (hence, reliable), could be distinguished from "subjective" speculation, seen as the product of imagination and opinion (hence, unreliable).

This, said Grant, was the basis of the "modern project," which sought to restructure *all* of life, whether the natural environment or human spheres such as the political, economic, labour, or social orders, on the basis of these principles. In other words, a useful notion for the employment of rational thought and argument was being asked to do much, much more. In the pre-Christian Greek tradition, he noted, it was believed that reason would enable people to lead better lives; in the modern project, reason became a tool to impose the human will upon both the natural and human orders. Furthermore, one of the prime movers of western society since the early middle ages, Christianity, had become less and less relevant to the structures and policies shaping everyday life. An instrumental, rationalist, mechanistic view of the world began replacing the view of nature as God's handiwork. And the technology ("making" and "doing") which it spawned to recreate the world was also mechanistic. In short, Grant concluded, the modern technological drive and the modern project were essentially one and the same.

The modern project, this technological drive, was both revolutionary and destructive. Rejected, Grant noted, were such "old-fashioned" concepts as mythic consciousness and religious/philosophical "systems" of meaning and morality. "Living" nature had been neutralized, no longer bound by religious or metaphysical taboos against its exploitation. Spirituality had been replaced with a view which saw the world as "raw material" upon which technology, dominated by (scientific) instrumental reason, could work its will. Henceforth, there would be a kind of Nietzschean "will to power" behind this drive to dominate nature through reason, a "will" that was to be exercised in total *freedom* from restraint.

Ever since, in the modern project, the ideals of modern technology and freedom have been linked as the surest way to improve the quality of life. Technological development (and an almost total faith in *technique*) has become the primary law, and continuous expansion and change the norm. Freedom means the absence of limits — everything is do-able, make-able, re-place-able, and/or exchange-able. That which does not accord with the ideals of modern technology and freedom will eventually be cast aside.

These were the views uncritically accepted by those who shaped and defined the direction of Canada's institutions in the nineteenth century (and continue to define them to the present). And why not? They had before them the inspiring example of Great Britain, the world's leading economic, industrial, and military power. By the second half of the nineteenth century, Canada's next-door neighbour, the United States, was also well on the way to joining the world's elite of powerful nations. How could Canada's leaders not have been impressed and inspired to follow the lead of two of the world's most powerful countries, both English-speaking, as are the dominant elements in Canada?

Yet there were signs warning of serious consequences of moving in this direction. The British enclosure movement of the eighteenth century, for example, was an early indication of the costs to ordinary people of this brave new world. New agricultural techniques displaced peasants from their land by enclosing their holdings into rational, squared-off units. Specialized crops replaced traditional peasant diversities of use. Furthermore, traditional crafts, technologies, and customs were displaced by new industrial technologies. But supporters of the new liberal, capitalist order saw the displacement of these people and their way of life as temporary, necessary, and inevitable dislocations on the way to a better future.

Given liberal notions of progress (linked to technological, industrial development) prevalent in the nineteenth century, it is no surprise then that Canada's leaders paid scant attention to the impacts of such phenomena as the enclosure movement but strove instead to emulate the "successes" of Britain and the

United States. In fact, British-Canadian leaders employed principles similar to those of the enclosure movement in their treatment of North America's Native peoples and placed them on reserves once their rights to their lands had been extinguished with treaties. Since then, the path of industrialization across the country, driven and fuelled by modern technology, has been relentless. Not only have all of Canada's leaders, whether Liberal, Progressive Conservative, NDP, Reform or otherwise, accepted industrialization based on modern technology as the path to "progress," but the "will to technology," as Grant called it, has invaded every aspect of life, and has swept away and/or marginalized all obstacles in its path.

This invasion is manifest in the existence of an immense governmental, industrial, corporate network which, Grant argued, exists in Canada because the nature and extent of modern technology is such that it can only function successfully in a world of large public and private corporations, precluding other and possibly "nobler" forms of community. In short, for its survival, modern technology requires the creation of global systems of research, development, and trade capable of exerting total control. And these systems, he concluded, are incompatible with sovereign states such as Canada.

This need for large systems is well illustrated by the way in which modern technology pervades people's "outer" lives, whether in how they use land, build houses, shape their cities, transport themselves and their goods, or make their livelihoods. Cars cannot be driven without a huge, complex system which includes the oil, mining, and manufacturing industries, wholesale and retail enterprises, governments, international alliances, and transportation networks. A car is no simple creation. Nor, as the ice storm of 1998 in Quebec showed, is something as basic as electricity, which involves cables, lines, power stations (coal, oil or nuclear-fired or hydro-dams), pipelines, government policy, and so forth. Virtually no facet of modern life, even something as simple as turning on a light or answering a telephone, can escape the pervasive influence of technology.

But it goes deeper. In a recent study of human happiness, Mark Kingwell has argued:

> In the culture at large we now pursue the basic philosophical question of happiness — what is the life worth living? — with a decidedly *technological* bent. We believe we can settle the question of life's value with the precise tools of scientific reason, and alleviate any lack of happiness with the products of scientific genius. . . .
>
> Let us say, then that the central idea in the modern manufacture of contentment is what we might call the Machine of Better Living. The Machine of Better Living is a thing or program that embraces the powerful temptation, variously conceived today, of an algorithm technique, process, code or prescription that will *render us happy*. I am using the word "machine" to imply not only technological devices of various kinds, literal machines, but also the entire internal logic of power and control associated with the modern triumph of instrumental reason, the rationality of means to ends: metaphorical machines. The Machine of Better Living could be a drug, a program of therapy, or even just a material object that we invest with significance, which we think will cure what ails us. *(If only I had a BMW. . . .)*

The Machine of Better Living "tell[s] us a great deal about what is for sale in the culture but little about what is of value." This view, he concludes, contrasts sharply with traditional western notions of happiness:

... for the ancient philosophers there could be no happiness that was not rooted in the demanding task of systematic self-examination. The idea of happiness embraced far more than the experience of simple pleasure or contentment; instead it included the idea of rational satisfaction, a sense (as Aristotle said) "that one is doing and faring well." For these thinkers that meant a life of ethical action, manifest in a well-formed virtuous character, and the associations typical of the good life: political community, friendship, family.

Happiness was understood not as contentment or personal salvation or even unconditional love, but as "ethical self-approval."

Kingwell's argument underscores the fact that modern technology with its focus on instrumental reason *(technique)* intrudes into people's very being: their "inner" lives, their physical, mental, and spiritual realities. Harold Innis has pointed out that modern technology, through such mechanisms as the print media, radios, televisions, and computers (the latter whose widespread use he did not live to see), has begun to take control of the "apparatus of symbolization" and is shaping the way people view and value themselves, others, and the world around them. Their souls are being infiltrated and modified by modern technology, the technology born of the Enlightenment, the technology with which its practitioners sought to master the planet. In fact, as mankind nears the twenty-first century, the basic "stuff" of humanity — their chemical and neural makeup — is being examined, manipulated, altered, and recreated. Scientists are mapping human genetic structures, setting up the brave new world of genetic engineering/re-creation, which modern medicine hopes will eradicate many of the physical and medical problems currently experienced by human beings.

The price for this Nietzschean bargain has been steep. The

Enlightenment dream of nature as the great teacher, that everything that humans need to know can be derived by discovering the laws of nature, is leaving humanity without a moral compass. As Grant noted, "values cannot be discovered in 'nature' because in the light of modern science nature is objectively conceived as indifferent to value."

In addressing what he saw as a major flaw of capitalism, Joseph Schumpeter took the idea of the Nietzschean bargain in another direction:

> Capitalism creates a rational frame of mind which, having destroyed the moral authority of so many other institutions, in the end turns against its own. The bourgeois finds to his amazement that the rationalist attitude does not stop at the credentials of kings and popes, but goes on to attack private property and the whole scheme of bourgeois values.

His assertion is valid. It was only a matter of time before the tools of the Enlightenment, systematic doubt, instrumental reason, and quantification, tools which had ridiculed, attacked, and rendered second-rate all values but those of the modern project, would be turned not only on the products of the Enlightenment but on the Enlightenment's modern project itself.

Michael Polanyi has argued that, in early twentieth-century continental Europe, this is precisely what happened. Followers of the Enlightenment view of reason used its own critical methods to attack and negate its own principles, to call into question the validity of both philosophical doubt and instrumental reason. Having spent two centuries negating and relativizing all other systems, many Europeans found themselves in a moral vacuum, embracing a profound skepticism about the validity of any value system. This mindset, Polanyi reminds us, is called *nihilism,* that is, the rejection of all established institutions,

144

laws, and ways of perceiving.

Grant too has pointed out that the liberal modern project, with its "will to technique" and its rejection of all other value systems but itself, leads to nihilism. It was Nietzsche, he says, who most clearly saw the implications of the "chaos" resulting from the modern project:

> For Nietzsche the fundamental experience for man was apprehending what is chaos; values were what we creatively willed in the face of chaos by overcoming the impotence of the will which arises from the recognition of the consequences of historicism.

In other words, the free and allegedly creative "will" becomes the only value, with no moral restrictions and no constraints on human action. Everything becomes relative, and everything becomes accept-able and even do-able, but very little has meaning. People have begun to exclude the mysteries of beauty and love (which Grant defined as the recognition of "authentic otherness"). Grant notes that the liberal tradition narrows the horizon to an "unmitigated reliance on technique":

> Therefore as our liberal horizons fade in the winter of nihilism, and as the dominating amongst us see themselves with no horizon except their own creating of the world, the pure will to technology (whether personal or public) more and more gives sole content to that creating. In the official intellectual community this process has been called "the end of ideology." What that phrase flatteringly covers is the closing down of willing to all content except the desire to make the future by mastery, and the closing down of all thinking which transcends calculation. . . . We now move towards the position where technological progress becomes itself the sole context within which all that is other to it must attempt to be present.

There is little meaning other than technology and what it purports to be able to do for the individual. He suggests that people may know of alternatives to this all-encompassing invasion of their being and loss of meaning only through "intimations of deprival." Deeper meaning and higher purpose seem to have disappeared.

Political scientist Charles Taylor uses the term "horizon of significance" to denote that which humans need for *self-fulfilment,* the latter a concept which he finds valuable because of its recognition of individual worth. He defines "horizon of significance" as "that without which creation loses the background that can save it from insignificance." That background, when one considers self-fulfilment for the individual, he says, must include two qualifiers: relationship to other human beings (dialogue), and the recognition of human connection to something bigger (more sacred) than mere human desires. He explains: "independent of my will there is something noble, courageous, and hence significant in giving shape to my life." However, liberalism's focus on self-fulfilment without boundaries, without the above-mentioned qualifiers, threatens people with a loss of meaning, a "flattened" world where there ". . . aren't very meaningful choices because there aren't any crucial issues." In other words, we end up with "nihilism," which Taylor defines as "a negation of all horizons of significance."

If the liberal, technological mindset, the modern project, takes us all to the homogenized future of the new global order and creates this wasteland of meaning, can something as quaint as national sovereignty or pride in one's unique country, region, or community be anything more than outdated nostalgia or idle dreaming?

This question has particular resonance for Canadians, situated as they are next to the United States, which, Grant argued, in the late eighteenth century, became the scene of a radical experiment, namely, the attempt to implement the Enlightenment's modern project. The United States, he noted, was a good laboratory for this project; it was a country in which Old European traditions and institutions had shallow roots. Thus, when its founding leaders gave the country its shape in the 1770s and 1780s, they were free to implement the new liberal philosophy without much competition from other ideals. The United States would be the frontier for the modern project; there would be complete freedom, the freedom to tame nature into the promised, modern, technological land of the future. Anything and everything that stood in its way, whether the original Native people or the natural environment, could and would be swept aside. For Grant, the clearest examples of this spirit was the space program: sending people into space for no intrinsic purpose but to prove that it could be done, that even outer space could, and should, be subjected to human control and domination.

Such philosophizing about the nature of the modern project may appear to many Canadians as mere naysaying and evidence of a refusal to embrace the future (and "progress"). After all, is not the "success" of America's liberal experiment manifest in the country's "heroic" remaking of the physical landscape to suit the technological imperative, with apparently obvious improvements to human material and physical well-being? Has this path not been of great benefit to Canada and its people? And is not such progress now happening worldwide? Indeed, under the leadership of the United States, there has been a global spread of the technologies created by the Enlightenment world view, of the focus on instrumental reason, of the ideal of the domination of the natural environment and of human nature, and of liberal, democratic ideals. Is the distribution of such benefits to more and more people not a good thing?

From some points of view, the answer is clearly yes. But the cost of this "progress" has been high. In his *Lament* of 1965, Grant believed that the modern project had already cost Canada its sovereignty, that the country had already been "swallowed up" by the American empire. However, the issue is (and was, even in 1965) more complicated than simply the disappearance of Canada into the American empire. World history since World War II shows that the United States has been merely the leading voice in the unfolding of the modern project. The modern project is larger than any particular country. Canada, most other western countries, and many Asian and South American countries have been embracing the modern project as avidly as the United States.

The extent to which the modern project has been accepted is illustrated by the current drive to the globalization of the modern, technological, industrial world-view, which, in Grant's terms, is nothing less than the globalization of the modern project. While the support of American political and economic elites is still a crucial component of its successful implementation, the modern project is obviously not the product or the ambition of any one country. In fact, real power and control over ways of living and styles of making and creating cultural and technological artifacts is now devolving from countries to an international elite which dominates an increasingly smaller number of trans-national corporations and their political allies.[1]

The main concern for Canadians in the spread of the modern project, therefore, should not be their historical suspicion of all things American. The fear of being subsumed by the

United States is merely a smokescreen for a larger issue. Rather, Canadians should be concerned about the spread of the modern project itself, about the imperial power of trans-national corporations which are the main carriers of this ideal, and about the manner in which Canada's governments and corporate elites continue to encourage it.

Countering the imperialism of trans-national corporations is no easy task. In many ways, their power is both more subtle and extensive than that of traditional nation-state empires because they lack the political and military characteristics usually associated with traditional empires, such as definable boundaries and imperial or colonial territories. But like traditional empires, they rely upon networks of communication (any and all forms of interaction among peoples) for success and survival. Indeed, history has shown that powerful empires, from the first ones of Sumer and China, to those of early twentieth-century European nation states, succeeded because they exercised dominance and control over systems of communication, whether these were in trade, finance, transportation, military affairs, or technology.

Empires have consistently striven to develop ever more sophisticated mechanisms of power and control (communications systems) to ensure both the continuation and potential spread of their dominance, especially in the face of rival imperial systems. In the last two hundred years, under the impetus of the modern project, there has been an unprecedented expansion of imperial power. Through most of human history, while communication systems developed ever more capability for control, one characteristic remained virtually unchanged: goods, people, and information moved at roughly the same speed. By 1900, driven by Enlightenment concepts of nature and technology and by liberal, capitalist ideologies, leading western, industrial and military nations had introduced and then spread around the world railways, telegraph systems, electricity, internal combustion engines, and wireless transmission. These forms of communication radically altered human concepts of space and time, and gave those who controlled them unprecedented capacity for dominance. By the beginning of the twentieth century, using their monopoly over these new powerful forms of communication, a handful of European countries and the United States carved up the world into colonies and/or spheres of influence.

The European/American, global, imperial system came apart after 1945 and most of the former colonies gained "independence." But the European/American need and desire for the "benefits" (outside sources of food, resources, and markets) of empire did not end. To meet this need, imperialism changed its appearance into what Kwame Nkrumah of Ghana called "neo-colonialism," by which he meant that traditional colonialism (European/American nation-state dominance of non-western countries) had been replaced by the economic dominance of trans-national corporations. Europeans and Americans, he pointed out, would be able to continue living in the style to which they had become accustomed.

Nkrumah is correct. As Harold Innis has noted in his evaluation of the development of Canada's economic history, in the modern, nation-state imperial systems (such as that to which Canada's nineteenth-century colonies belonged), economic and technological gaps between imperial powers and colonies had increased exponentially because the contribution of "staples" (i.e., food and natural resource raw materials) from the colonies had enabled the imperial powers to industrialize ever more quickly while the economies of the colonies remained primarily focused on non-industrial "staples" production. When colonialism ended, former colonies were still economically dependent on trade with their former colonial overlords because their limited industrial infrastructures could not compete with them to produce sufficient quantities of the cheaply priced goods upon which they now relied. After confederation, Canada's trade reliance on Britain and later on the United States was a clear case in point.

In the aftermath of World War II, nation-state colonialism evolved quite naturally into trans-national corporate imperialism. Today's transportation and electronic technologies, which are capable of moving information, goods, and money swiftly around the globe, are far more powerful than the communication systems of the former nation-state empires. Because privately controlled trans-nationals are capable of manufacturing parts in one or more countries, assembling them in others, and selling the finished product wherever the most profits can be made, they locate their operations wherever there are the fewest environmental, labour, or financial restrictions. They can whisk money around the globe at a speed beyond the control of national governments.

This unprecedented private power of trans-national corporations is also accompanied by a general lack of accountability to the general good, whether to people or to nature. The corporations are primarily answerable to shareholders whose nationalities are irrelevant and whose major interest is as much profit as possible, with few questions about the means used to achieve it. At least the former nation-state imperial powers had electorates to which they had to pay some attention. Many of the poorer, former colonies are, by and large, now worse off than under nation-state imperialism.

Unfortunately, today's subjects of trans-national, corporate imperialism, whether in the poorer countries or in the industrialized world, are displaying an unprecedented lack of resistance to this imperial dominance. Canada's political leaders, leading think-tanks, and many of its academics, now that the cold war has ended, are far too uncritical in accepting this new global ideology, as if world-wide economic integration controlled by trans-national corporatism is both natural and good. Speaking of an emerging and prosperous "global consumer culture," free of want, connected by "global communications" produced by "global technologies" for the "global village," they predict that, as long as Canadians remain "competitive" and allow the marketplace as directed by these corporate entities to operate unimpeded by government policy or restrictions (a state of affairs deemed as "natural" and "right"), their prosperity will be assured.

Are we to trust such prognostications of "progress?" Almost certainly not, for as sociologist Max Dublin has pointed out:

> Predictions can lead us to abandon something of the present — something "better" that we have known, valued, understood, and lived with over the years — in favor of something "better" that we neither know, nor value, nor properly understand but that, we are told, will be a great good in the future. We hasten to disassociate ourselves from worthwhile endeavors that enrich our lives in large part because their demise has been predicted and we do not want to be "left behind."

But advocates seldom tell people from what they will be "left behind." *Utne Reader* writer Jay Walljasper, paraphrasing United States' economist Hazel Henderson, notes that the futurists' predicting is much less a science than an agenda,

... which more often than not, meshes with the interests of
the corporations that pay handsomely for their services. Big
business has invested heavily in new technology and global
trade, so of course they want to hear that those are the things
that will matter in the 21st century. And that's what futurists
tell them.

Canadians must leave the welcoming party for the new global
order, although it will not be easy, since seldom in the history of
humanity have subjects embraced imperialism as eagerly as in
our time.[2]

In Canada, the dream has been powerful and seductive
enough to prevent the country's elites (as noted above) from
heeding the (1940) Rowell Sirois Commission's caution about
the consequences of foregoing self-sufficiency and tying Canada's economic future to global forces. Nietzsche once com-
mented that "big fish eat little fish." What will happen to countries such as Canada when the big fish, after a frenzy of feeding,
discover that they have run out of little fish to consume? Will
the edifice of trans-national, corporate empires come crashing
down? Robert Heilbroner has warned:

> There exists no effective political counterforce to undertake
> the fiscal, monetary, and regulatory moves that might be re-
> quired to stabilize production if th[e] trans-national structure
> should ever begin to shake. We are in much the same condi-
> tion of helplessness with regard to maintaining or repairing
> the flow of trans-national production as we were with respect
> to maintaining our domestic flows of output in the 1930s.

He notes that 350 corporations have combined sales equal to
one-third of the Gross National Product of the entire industrial
world; if this trans-national "superstructure" ever collapses, there
will be massive, global instability. And still Canada's leaders

continue to tie the country's future to this system.

But even if this catastrophe were to be avoided, the price of trans-national, corporate imperialism wedded to the modern project may still be too high. Around the globe, where there used to be many peoples, many worlds, many "natures," many freedoms, and many histories, Enlightenment science, technology, and industrialization, and the consequent commodification of life, have created increasing sameness and homogenization. At the external level, this destruction can be seen in the loss of identifiable natural and human environments. At the internal level, all across the globe, identities are merging, evidenced by the rapid loss of indigenous languages and their replacement by mass media culture.[3] As Innis has noted, the quicker the dissemination of goods and information, the greater the disruption to local cultures and to the peoples whose identity arises from their local-ness. Fewer and fewer regions or people have the power to stand apart or to control their identities. Current dissemination of information and "news" about world events, for example, is controlled by a small (and shrinking) number of agencies and corporate communications empires. Modern technology has minimized the rich diversity among people, a diversity which, problematic at times, nevertheless defines being human.

Countries and peoples attempting to oppose trans-national, corporate dominance appear to be fighting a losing battle. Usually, they conclude that they have little option but to industrialize and to adopt western technological methods if they are to remain free from poverty. But as the Canadian experience shows, the adoption of the modern technological, industrial way of life requires vast sums of capital, and, of course, this capital can only come from the sources which have it. As a result, newly industrializing parts of the world quickly amass huge debts to the industrialized countries' governments and banks which direct the policies of organizations such as the World Bank and IMF whose purpose ostensibly is to "assist" countries to "develop." Rather than recreating the wheel and starting from scratch themselves, newly industrializing countries adopt the easier (Canadian) alternative, and allow the trans-national corporations to set up branch plants. In so doing, however, they lose control over production. Modern technology is, thus, a hand-maiden to neo-colonial, trans-national corporate imperialism. Countries adopting this approach become bound not only to western, liberal, industrial values and practices but also to those who control them.[4] They lose their traditional, local ways of life, as well as control of their destinies.

This universal homogenization is spelling not only the end of government systems as we have known them, but also the national policies which can protect local cultures. International financial institutions and trans-national corporations, which operate independently from modern state structures (they are not democratically elected), and which are accountable for their actions only to their shareholders, are being handed more and more power by the world's most powerful governments in the name of government downsizing and deregulation. Canadian federal and provincial governments meekly accept the judgments of bond-rating agencies, for example, and adjust their economic and financial policies according to the prescriptions of these foreign, not-accountable-to-ordinary-people organizations. As Ursula Franklyn has pointed out, governments are abdicating their responsibility of protecting the good of the commonwealth and of administering justice on behalf of all. Instead, they are focussing on making the "world a safe place for technology" and for those who control and profit from it. While some cynics and neo-liberal ideologues may applaud the dying of modern governments, the alternative is frightening. Instead of desiring the end of governments, Canadians ought to be calling them back to their true function and responsibility.

In the same vein, Grant argued that the liberal ideal of equality could soon mean "equality in 'primary goods' for a majority in the heartlands of empire," but exclude equality for those who are "inconvenient," who are too "... weak to enforce contracts — the imprisoned, the mentally unstable, the un-born, the aged, the defeated, and sometimes even the morally nonconforming." He worried that a mean-spirited reduction of justice in favour of power had developed in the technical age. The Darwinian intolerance exhibited by neo-liberalism bears out his fear. In such an environment, democracy is a sham, and the notion of Canada as a sovereign country seems nonsensical.

It is not being suggested that this growing dominance of the technological mindset of the modern project, controlled and administered by trans-national corporations, was planned, that Canada's leaders in the mid-nineteenth century could have foreseen that the liberal vision would lead to this end. They saw the liberal, technological, capitalist ideal primarily as a way to attain self-government from Britain and to provide themselves and their offspring with a better material life. The British North America Act of 1867, which established a government mod-elled on the British, liberal ideals was, as Donald Creighton has noted, hammered out in a few weeks, demonstrating near una-nimity among colonial leaders about the kind of country they wished to create. Since then, few political leaders, including most of those from the left (the CCF/NDP tradition), have seri-ously challenged the modern project or offered significant alternatives to the ideology of liberal, technological, industrial growth.

Until recently, there was a significant number of thinkers who offered Marxism-Leninism as an alternative, who pointed out that capitalism was an exploitive system which had to be replaced by one which allowed for the free creative activity of each individual. As early as 1916, Lenin identified the power of corporate capitalism to exploit colonies to produce wealth for rich Europeans. But as Grant noted in his *Lament,* both Marx and Lenin accepted the necessity of industrialization and of the technological dominance of nature. This should not be surprising. As John Ralston Saul has pointed out, Marxism, fascism, and the marketplace (liberalism) are all "corporatist, managerial, and hooked on technology." How could it be not so? They developed from the same Enlightenment stock.

At the heart of the problem of modernity, therefore, is the core philosophy which drives countries such as Canada. Canadians who argue only about such matters as the independence of its economic structures, the form of its industrial development, the nature of its social programs, or the extent of foreign investment — as important as these issues may be — are missing the point. The liberal, industrial, technological society is based on a world-view which embraces an exploitive approach to the natural environment and an homogenizing tendency with respect to lifestyle and culture. It also threatens individual human expression and freedom (despite its promise to do the opposite), and it opens the door to nihilism. Canada's current commitment to globalization, particularly in the market-place, reduces local variety not only by permitting the power over production and distribution to devolve to a handful of corporations, but also by allowing these self-same corporations control over

157

the whole range of communications, over the marketing of values and ideas. Not just people's bodies, but their hearts, minds, and souls are being subjected to manipulation and control.

This is the real issue that Canadians must consider in discussions about free trade agreements, "Team Canada" missions, the MAI, or the new economic global order. In the 1960s, Grant was probably correct when he lamented that subservience to these values had already destroyed Canada's sovereignty. While the products of the Canadian arts/literary establishment do not necessarily define Canadian identity, it is instructive to see which cultural forms Canadians tend to embrace. Pulp literature, American television and radio, American styles in fashion and architecture, and all the household and personal gadgets produced by the technological, industrial system sell well in Canada. Everyday life differs little from that in the United States. As we approach the twenty-first century, it is time to stop dealing with peripheral issues. If Canadians ignore the core philosophy and the world-view which dominates contemporary Canada, the only serious debate that will occupy its leaders will be the manner in which Canadians march to an homogenized future, not if they will.

At the end of *Lament for a Nation,* Grant implied that it may be "old-fashioned," even "reactionary," to "resist this inevitable trend." Nonetheless, he mourned the lack of serious debate about, and the liberal dismissal of, traditional concepts such as Truth, Goodness, and Justice, and their replacement with an obsessive, blind acceptance of ideas about the conquest of nature, of profit, and of an open-ended, relativistic morality. In short, he was saddened by uncritical acceptance of the modern project.

Although his lament may strike a responsive chord, nostalgia and a desire to return to past ways of thinking and behaving are not healthy ways to deal with the country's present situation. As can be seen with the misguided neo-liberal ideology, the desire to invoke past glories often ignores elements which even adherents would not likely wish to repeat. Grant's sadness about the fading of many Judaeo-Christian and Greek (particularly Platonic) values that have shaped the west for centuries and their replacement by the current, arbitrary, ethical standards of liberalism, conveniently overlooks that many elements of these traditional standards, vigorously promoted by the elites of the past, often produced war, bloodshed, and intolerance. A return to such patterns of thinking might also be a return to the male-defined hierarchies and patriarchies whose practices created much of Canada's present crisis. At times, Grant was overly fond of things British, as if that tradition were somehow purer than the United States' liberal dream which, ironically, was its natural offspring. John Locke was very English, as were the ideals of the United States' revolutionaries.

Nonetheless, Grant is correct in asserting that liberalism has no tolerance for traditional religious and philosophical concepts. Yet liberalism cannot eradicate the desire to believe in something transcendent, lasting and solid, the desire that underlies many of the world's great religions and that is the basis for Taylor's concept of "horizon of significance." The desire, because it is presently unmet in the lives of so many people, has resulted in wide-scale individual and social uncertainty, manifested by substance abuse, crime, suicide, and the other spiritual and environmental issues noted earlier. The liberal focus on continual change, on growth, and development creates a void that people then attempt to fill with even more change, growth, and development. Liberalism dissolves traditional concepts, inflames the desire for security, and offers only an open-ended, uncertain, de-natured, nihilistic future.

The desire for meaning and purpose is only partly offset by the toys, consumer products, and gadgets produced by the industrial system. Few Canadian homes are without VCRs, microwave ovens, computers, food processors, hair dryers, answering machines, or other such products. People are fed so much pap from the media, have so many distractions, and are kept so busy scraping up money to pay for what they believe that they need that they have little time to rebel, even if they were inclined to do so. We can only agree with E.F. Schumacher's lament that ". . . fewer and fewer people can be real people."

This is not to say that most Canadians are uncaring. Take the problem of pollution, for example. Few Canadians endorse environmental destruction or the despoliation of nature. Many, in fact, support strong, and even costly, measures that would ensure a healthy world for their children. Yet they are all expected, even required (for survival) to work hard and to buy into a "lifestyle" (now just another "commodity") which, because of its wastefulness in combination with other "lifestyles," effectively destroys the earth. Canadians' collective vision and collective practices need repair, especially because the present focus is on individual desire rather than on overall good.

Ultimately, the well-being of Canada's communities depends upon an awareness of collective responsibility that remains ethically grounded in humanity's creaturely relationship to the natural environment. The continuation of the present path is a sure recipe for disaster. As Ursula Franklin has said: "We must protest until there is a change in the structures and practices of the *real world of technology* [emphasis mine], for only then can we hope to survive as a global community." Canadians must

160

move beyond the blandishments of a global, consumer culture that seductively offers a better life for all. As Franklin concludes, future generations, if present paths are not abandoned, are doomed to being little more than scavengers in an "unlivable techno-dump."

NOTES

1 Ironically, even as globalism spreads liberal values and there are increasing calls for the spread of democracy around the globe, the majority of the world's people are still denied constitutionally protected, individual rights and have little access to liberal democratic governments. Instead, as they witness liberalism uprooting their ways of life, they are finding themselves enslaved to trans-national, corporate power, which in reality constitutes a new form of imperialism.

2 This, in spite of the fact that in the last twenty years the world's wealthiest twenty percent of people have seen their income double from thirty to sixty times that of the lowest twenty percent who live in dire poverty.

3 Peter Popham (*Vancouver Sun,* January 20, 1996) has estimated that about half of the world's current 6,000 languages could be lost in the next century by the takeover of what he calls the "transnational tongues" such as English, Spanish, and French.

4 This control devolves to a handful of countries, as evidenced by the fact that while 181 nations belong to the IMF, 6 of the world's leading nations contributed 43.1% of the fund's total 1997 income, with the US alone contributing 18%.

6

HEALTHY REGIONS
FOR A HEALTHY CANADA

I'm not being pessimistic at all. I think that
God will eventually destroy this technological
civilization. I'm very optimistic about that.
— George Grant

No wonder people are disaffected with our
governments. It's not that governments are
powerless, it's that they have ceased to use
their power to defend the public interest.
— Linda McQuaig, *The Cult of Impotence*

If, in the face of liberalism's homogenizing tendencies, Canadians wish to see their country survive as a distinct, sovereign
entity, they have little choice but to begin resisting the blandishments of the modern project. For a start, they will need to
redefine the links between federal, provincial, and regional
governments and systems, with far greater importance and
emphasis being placed on the regional level than is currently
the case.

A possible model for this direction was suggested more than half a century ago by the American philosopher of modernity, Lewis Mumford, whose thoughts on cities, regions, and planning are still relevant and useful. His ideal regions had three important characteristics. First of all, he argued, they should be geographically distinct, defined by land mass, climate, geologic structure, soil vegetation, animal life, and other such physical characteristics. Secondly, such regions should include people with a unique identity, distinguished by their laws, manners, customs, patterns of housing, architecture, village and city structures, and modifications of the landscape, and who shared gestures, dialects, and feelings. Finally, such regions should be "large enough to embrace a sufficient range of interests, [but] small enough to keep these interests in focus and to make them a focus of direct collective concern." Boundaries of such regions, he pointed out, were, of necessity, fluid.

Thirty years before Grant sounded his alarm, Mumford worried that the forces of imperialism and capitalism were laying waste many of the natural and human systems which had historically defined people. Distinctive regions were disappearing around the world. He warned: "We have reached the end of the journey, and in the main, we must retrace our steps, and region by region, learn to do intelligently and cooperatively what we hitherto did in such disregard of the elementary decencies of life." He is correct. Canadians must refocus on regional well-being, thinking, and living.

E.F. Schumacher argued much the same in *Small is Beautiful*. He noted that Switzerland, a relatively small country, contains more than twenty cantons, ". . . each of which is a kind of development district, with the result that there is a fairly even spread of population and of industry and no tendency towards the formations of excessive concentrations." India, on the other hand, because of its huge size, had concentrated development in a few metropolitan areas, with the result that the vast majority of people did not share the benefits, remained unemployed and poor, and drifted to the cities where they hoped to turn their fortunes around. "If the purpose of development is to bring help to those who need it most, each region or district within the country needs its own development." It was Schumacher's contention that appropriate development included at least the following: that workplaces ought to be created where people were presently living and not in the cities to which they tended to migrate, that the workplaces on average should be designed on a scale that did not require huge levels of "capital formation and imports," and "that production should be mainly from local materials and mainly for local use." Canada, unfortunately, with fewer people and an abundance of resources (hence, less dire poverty), has embarked on a path similar to the one followed by India.

Mexican activist Gustavo Esteva approaches the question of regional power from the political/cultural angle, and argues for more self-government and participation by people in their decisions. Advocates of the development model, he says, attempt to change

> . . . our basic values, our basic attitudes, our basic moral imperatives, and our practical attitudes, our ways of being, our very basic notion of what the good life is. [They] go deeper and deeper, to deeper layers of our souls, of our being, to teach us, to educate us in another attitude.

Under the influence of the growth and development model, people begin to mistrust their traditions, their communities, their families, and established ways of life. Instead, they are taught to put faith in governments, in experts, in scientists, in engineers, in planners:

> Development means starting on a road others know better, running towards a goal others have reached, racing up a one-way street. Development means sacrificing the environment and traditional customs to ever changing expert advice. Development promises enrichment, but for the overwhelming majority it has always meant the progressive modernization of their own poverty: growing dependence on guidance and management.

The price that people pay for placing their trust in leaders, experts, and/or bureaucrats is the loss of trust in themselves, in their neighbours, in their communities, and in their sense of how things should be. Esteva offers an antidote:

> We want to establish the rights of communities, the right of every community to govern itself, following its own definition of what a good life is, following its own rules, its own systems, its own traditions, but with a kind of limitation of communal power. We want a kind of protection for the person and a kind of protection for the community. We are convinced that the people must have in their hands their own government, their own spaces, their own ways of doing things, and there are just a few things that must be in the hands of the government at the capital.

Or, as Smithu Kothari argues, people must recover "access and control over forests, over lands, over waters. . . ." Rather than helping people, the top-down approach is multiplying their problems. People everywhere need to combine thinking from the bottom-up with current awareness of and knowledge about the inter-relatedness of all parts of the planet.

This is, of course, fine sounding rhetoric but current political reality works against such ideas. As noted above in the discussion of the Greater Victoria area, British Columbia's provincial government has established a system of local government in which, once every three years, residents of towns, cities, and municipalities elect councils which have virtually unlimited power. They can amend their Official Community Plans (OCPs), Official Settlement Plans (OSPs) and zoning bylaws (which define land use, building types and sizes, and so forth) at will and at any time, with no legislated or formal requirement to respect the wishes or input from residents. This makes it impossible for communities (at least for the small number of their citizens who remain interested) to create meaningful long-term visions or to have any security that such visions will have much shelf-life.

In reality, the provincial government's rules defining OCPs and zoning bylaws in British Columbia (and most provinces) are actually designed to encourage rapid growth and development, regardless of popular opinion about such concepts. The province requires, for example, that OCPs, OSPs, and zoning bylaws designate (in effect, set aside) land for future uses and densities greater than current ones, assuming that "build-out" of "developable" land will require dipping into a pool of new or "raw" (often agricultural) land ready to be rezoned and developed. As a result, speculation in land continues unabated, and local politics often degenerates into cat and mouse games over zoning and land-use issues among entrepreneurs (developers), local government staff, politicians, and citizens. It takes only one growth and development council (a few short weeks!) to develop land-use policies which can forever change the face of a community. And residents can do nothing to stop this, other than on election day once every three years. At the local level of government, where people have the most to lose, they have virtually no power. Resident recognition of this reality accounts for the low voter turnouts in city, town, and municipal elections.

To overcome their sense of powerlessness, citizens can attempt a number of things. For one thing, they can create "grassroots" mechanisms to speak out and try to influence decisions affecting their communities. Secondly, they can develop long-term visions for sustainability, mandated and underwritten by provincial and federal legislation.

First of all, with respect to "grassroots" mechanisms, there are two major kinds. One is "special interest" groups, dedicated to particular issues or philosophies such as education, forestry, agriculture, poverty, crime, etc. Such groups can be effective because they usually cut across political party labels and ideology, but their narrow focus and tendency not to address the larger economic, social, and political elements which underlie most issues is a serious shortcoming. And because of this narrow focus, they are also easy targets for opponents.

Residents can also organize into "grassroots" neighbourhood/village groups, similar to traditional ratepayer associations which, through regular newsletters and meetings, can educate residents about and lead them to take common action on zoning, (future) planning, and/or facilities/services issues in their area. They can establish visions for their neighbourhoods and work to enshrine them in municipal bylaws. They can explore the relationship of their communities to adjoining ones and the manner in which those jurisdictions deal with similar concerns. They have the advantage over "special interest" groups in that they can cover a wide range of issues relevant to people's everyday lives. Such groups can also interact with "special interest" groups such as those described above to promote a wider education for citizens.

"Special interest" and neighbourhood groups within one area, aligned with like-minded groups across the province, the country, even the globe, may well be important to politics of the future. But there is a caution. Franklin Saige, for example, notes that many in the ecology movement idealize a future "global village," fiber-optically connected: "I see the technology encouraging in them precisely the way of relating to lived experience that has brought about the crisis they seek to alleviate." A global village (connected technologically by means such as the internet) is an oxymoron; by definition, a village is a place where people meet face to face. Ursula Franklin notes that the global village is a "pseudo-community" (a sales ploy by those who create, control, and distribute the technology) in which people who never meet have the illusion of being part of a community. People need real contacts, real community. Or, as Jane Jacobs says, not a global village, but a globe of villages.

The second way for citizens to overcome their feelings of powerlessness, namely, the development of long-term visions of sustainability, will be effective only if citizens can also persuade senior governments to provide the legislative mechanisms to ensure that these visions are enforceable. It is time to replace the current style of planning, a process which Professor H. Peter Oberlander, former director of the School of Regional and Community Planning at the University of British Columbia, has described as "negative" and "restrictive," designed to "prevent the worst things from happening," one that shies away form long-term perspectives, but creates an uncoordinated landscape because it rezones, regulates, and allows building on a piece-meal basis. Instead, Canadians need to create long-term visions and "appropriate" planning techniques, supported legislatively, to ensure the implementation of plans to carry out such visions.

This is not a new idea. In the last decade, for example, residents in the Niagara Peninsula, the Ramsay Lake Watershed near Sudbury, and an 80-kilometer stretch of the South Saskatchewan River Valley have, by means of extensive public input, created hundred-year visions, based on the concept of visualizing what the area would be like in one hundred years if the principles of sustainability, preservation of natural life and features, and human cohabitation were factored in. Criteria for a complete environment that would ensure permanent livability for both human and natural environments (ultimately, one and the same) were established. In the case of the Ramsay Lake area, this meant letting nature recover, while in the case of the South Saskatchewan River it meant preserving its present diversity. The advantage of developing long-range perspectives is that self-interest diminishes because participants will not be around in one hundred years, and the needs of their descendants can take priority.

Integral to this view of planning is what Mumford has called the "ecology of the human community." He notes that the human species, and indeed all species, can only survive as part of a system of essential conditions: people depend upon a permanently sustainable relationship between people (their cultures, history, traditions, and sustenance activities) and nature (topography, soil, climate, flora, and fauna). And as Ursula Franklin has observed, nature is variable, not static or mechanistic as assumed by the (instrumental) rational planning methods and the technological model of twentieth-century land-use planning which, she notes, has "design[ed] nature *out* of much of our lives." The preservation of nature with all of its unpredictable variables must always underlie visions of the future and the planning which follows. These principles must be supported legislatively and constitutionally so that present and future generations can be held accountable if they fail to meet the standards of long-term sustainability.

To allow for this symbiotic relationship between the natural environment and human activity (agricultural land, space for human habitation and employment, and heritage sites and sacred land), William Rees and Mathis Wackernagel have suggested that human occupation be tied to an "ecological footprint," that is, the amount of "land and water that would be required to support a defined human population and material standard indefinitely." They have calculated that 7 hectares of productive land and aquatic regions are needed to sustain the present consumption patterns of the average person in the West. They estimate, however, that the total productive area available in the world is only 1.5 hectares of land and .5 hectares of aquatic resources per person. To sustain western consumption patterns for all of the world's present population, humans would need the resources and waste-acceptance capacity of approximately three planets identical to earth. Clearly, Canadians (and human beings generally) do not have this option. For the good of both the planet and humanity, they must re-evaluate their commitment to liberal values of consumption, technology, and industrialization.

To live within a sustainable "ecological footprint," Canadians, along with the citizens of other western countries, must reconsider the manner in which they devise the forms and structures of human settlements. A key step would be to redefine the current hierarchy of human living arrangements from the bottom-up rather than the top-down. Instead of cities, the most important units should be neighbourhoods, sub-units of cities and towns, small enough (five to ten thousand people) to give each resident the possibility for significant involvement and control in governance and decision-making, particularly in areas such as land-use planning and taxation for local matters. Work places, shopping areas (especially for groceries), community centres, village greens, schools, churches, and residences should, as much as possible, be within walking distance of each other, implying a high degree of local ownership and control over everyday needs. Streets and roads should be redesigned to lie largely outside of neighbourhoods, protecting residents from traffic and noise, allowing roadways to be places "to be" rather than through which to move quickly. The key to workable neighbourhoods is making sure that communication networks enhance face-to-face contacts. Communication networks, planned by and for the local people, should be their servants rather than their masters. This approach to land-use as a public concern and responsibility counters the prevalent notion that the most profit from land and development, for a few, represents the best use for all. Canada may have been "built" on the notion of "free," "empty" land, to be exploited with little thought about consequences, but such thinking does not foster a sense of stewardship of neighbourhoods and regions.

Furthermore, there should be as much local control as possible over the basic needs of life — secure shelter, safe food, clean water, clean air, and clothing — if people are to make their living arrangements sustainable. A recent article in the *New Internationalist* noted: "The wealth of the world is the diversity of its localities and their ability to generate ways and means of living which fit their resources and suit their cultures." The word "economy" literally means "household management," implying that economies should not belong to trans-national, market forces that are presided over by a small minority for their private benefit, nor even to distant governments half way across a continent. They should belong as much as possible to the communities and regions where people actually live. The long-distance importation of products to meet basic needs is questionable from an environmental perspective, but it also means that money leaves regions and communities to pay for the imported products. Money that circulates locally, directed to meet local (especially basic) needs, does more for regional and community sustainability than that which leaves for the coffers of distant banks, corporations, or government bureaucracies.[1]

In this context, the role of Canadian cities and their relationship to adjoining regions must also be rethought. Despite the fact that cities are often viewed with misgiving, they must occupy a key place in the kind of sustainable and liveable regions envisioned above.

People's fear of cities is not surprising because historically cities have often exercised immense power and control over surrounding and neighbouring areas. In fact, the world's first cities, 5,000 years ago in ancient Mesopotamia, were created when subsistence living was displaced by reliance on outside sources (over which cities exercised control) for the essentials of survival such as food and raw materials. Before long, Mesopotamian urban spaces became so large that it became necessary for the city-dwellers to produce "manufactured" (literally hand-made) goods in exchange for these essentials. The larger the area outside of cities which they were able to dominate/ control and from which they could draw or trade for their basic necessities, the more they could expand their physical space and increase the range and complexity of the goods and ser-

vices which they produced. But subsequent widespread salina-
tion and desertification of the region showed clearly that there
was a huge cost attached to the technologically based expansion of Mesopotamian power and territory. As was the case with
the Sahara region of Africa centuries later or to the Aral Sea
region of the former USSR recently, Mesopotamian cities over-
used the natural capacity of the region as well as the capacity of
their technology to sustain their human population.

This reality underscores the paradoxical nature of cities.
On the one hand, cities have given the world trade, commerce,
and empires, and their creative energy has produced the so-
called "gifts of civilization": technology, religion, leisure, the
arts, philosophy, learning, etc.[2] On the other hand, they are in
many respects dead places, sustained by constant outside sup-
plies of "fresh blood," whether food, resources, or people. They
involve an ever-increasing alienation of people from the natural order. Jacques Ellul has gone so far as to argue that Cain
built his city to "force nature to follow his destiny, his destiny of
slavery and sin, and his revolt to escape from it." Cities, he
notes, replace peoples' subsistence living patterns and their
reliance on nature with man-made (usually rational) order.

Modern cities have also become problematic at the personal
level, the importance of the individual diminishing in propor-
tion to a city's size and population. While people from smaller
communities often find cities liberating from the traditional,
social, religious, and personal restraints of rural and small town
life, they also experience more loneliness and isolation. It is in
cities that alcoholism, prostitution, suicide, and crime become
major social problems.

Despite that reality, modern cities around the world continue to attract large numbers of people who, lured by the seduc-

tions of western, particularly American, television and the promise of the good life, hope to overcome the social, religious, and cultural strictures and poverty of rural life. All too often, instead of finding themselves in picturesque, American-style suburbs as portrayed in the global media (ideals which even few American suburbs can match), they become denizens of sprawling and ever-expanding shanty-towns, largely denuded of vegetation and suffering from poisoned air, soil, and water.

Because cities eliminate most of nature, life and work in the modern city have little of humanity's traditional connection to natural rhythms and cycles. A tree on a busy boulevard, a tiny park among high-rises, or Central Park in New York are reminders of how modern cities have restructured the natural environment by removing most plants and animals. Humanity's historical subservience to nature has been exchanged for servitude to constructed systems of order and control, to the demands of industry and technology. As Ellul notes: ". . . technique adapts man to a world of steel." Unfortunately, the survival of modern cities increasingly depends upon this ever-growing alienation between worker and work, between the man-made and natural environments.

Still, many proponents of the modern project are optimistic about the future of such modern cities (in which they do not have to live day after day). Syndicated columnist Gwynne Dyer has argued that the paths of urban expansion, economic growth, and individual well-being are parallel. In the long run, he asserts, humanity will be better off in modern cities, even ones such as Mexico City, Beijing, and Singapore, which, he says, will overcome their social, economic, and environmental problems to match eventually the "progress" of "successful" cities such as Tokyo and New York.

This rosy view ignores that while some rural refugees are fleeing the "countryside" because they wish to leave traditional ways of life, just as many are being forced to leave because their homes and livelihoods are being destroyed by forms of modernity such as dams, mines, industrial forestry, or agribusiness. Dyer's view of the city ignores the biggest threat to humanity, namely, diminishing food-production capacity around the globe because of urbanization, the loss of arable land, and the pollution and decrease of potable water. If current trends continue, what will Mr. Dyer's urban folk eat and drink?

Nonetheless, cities are here to stay. In fact, in the type of regions towards which Canadians should aspire, cities will, and should, play a key role in providing the "gifts of civilization," whether technology or other cultural products. The creation of these gifts is fundamental to human interaction with the natural environment, even of human survival. It should, therefore, be clearly stated that it is not cities per se nor the "gifts of civilization," whether technology or culture, that have brought humanity to its present predicament. The problem is with the modern project's approach to technology, with its exploitive view of nature, whether human or other. As Schumacher insists, technology is crucial to human identity, as long as it is appropriate: that is, it does not rob people of dignity, the natural environment of sustainability, or humanity of useful remunerative activity. In the Canada of the future, cities must and will have a key role to play.

But because the creation of cities displaces local self-sufficiency and self-reliance in food and resources, and because the seduction of globalization leads to the creation of cities and suburban regions so large that they can no longer be sustained according to the principles described by Mumford, Canadians need to rethink the scale and nature of their cities. The size of cities and regions must not go beyond their geographically defined distinctiveness and "carrying capacity," nor should they extend beyond the unique culture and humanly created attributes which distinguish them from other cities and regions. If regions are defined so that they are large enough to provide for the basic necessities of the people who live in them, and contain neighbourhoods small enough to maintain citizen involvement and interest, we have a useful limiting factor for the size and structure of cities. Properly sized cities will consume fewer resources (e.g., higher densities requiring less energy), produce less pollution (e.g., more efficient modes of transportation), cost less in real dollars (e.g., infrastructure, health, and education economies of scales), and use land more responsibly than suburban or gentrified rural areas.

Canada is nowhere near such a situation. Instead, as the liberal value-system, directed by the imperatives of the modern project, eliminates distinctive ways of living, being, and thinking in favour of homogenization and globalization, the country's communities, cities, and regions are moving in the opposite direction, evolving into anonymous, de-natured clones, not only of each other but also of ones across North America. In this context, with no sense of living in unique places, most Canadians are finding concepts such as sovereignty and the Canadian identity too complex, too abstract to make sense.

For a unique Canadian sovereign state to survive, the cloning process must be reversed, and the distinctiveness and character of the islands making up the Canadian archipelago must be preserved along the lines suggested by people such as Mumford, Schumacher, Rees, and Wackernagel. The differences and uniqueness among people and the regions they inhabit, not their increasing sameness, are essential for the survival of Canada.

This assumes that Canadians want the survival of Canada. Indeed, as noted above and as polls are increasingly showing, more and more of them seem willing to accept the potential breakup of Canada. And who can blame them? Many, especially Native people and residents of Canada's poorer regions, have paid a steep price for confederation. Much of federal politics since 1867 has, as Grant tirelessly argued, favoured the liberal elites, whether in government, business, or the media, the very leaders whose present cozy relationship with the trans-national, corporate imperialists is threatening not only Canada's uniqueness but that of cultures and ways of life around the globe. Ironically, throughout Canada's history, they often used the banner of Canadian unity to further their own interests, successfully persuading their fellow citizens that a centralized federation rather than autonomous or quasi-independent regions would be to everyone's economic benefit and for the good of their country. Fewer Canadians are accepting this message. Unfortunately, the price for loss of faith may be the end of something many Canadians still treasure, namely, their country.

The political and economic elites who run this country have largely themselves to blame for this public skepticism. In the process of convincing Canadians that they were building a wonderful new society, they created political and bureaucratic structures which now are so entrenched that instead of unifying Canadians around the country's institutions, they have become a major obstacle to creating the environment necessary for keeping Canada together. Alan Cairns, in a 1977 article, noted that Canada's leaders "created [in 1867] competitive political and bureaucratic elites at two levels of government endowed with an impressive array of jurisdictional, financial, administrative, and political resources to deploy in their pursuit of their objectives." Since then, Canada's history has been "little more than the record of the efforts of the governing elites to pyramid their resources and of the uses to which they have put them." While the number of elected officials in Canada is quite small, the federal and provincial bureaucracies have become "large and powerful complexes of institutions and personnel with their own professional and personal interests, and their own official purposes for the . . . populations they govern." They have little incentive to see changes which may diminish their power: "The ministries, departments, agencies, bureaus, and field offices to which they daily report constitute partially self-contained entities, valued for their own sake, and possessed of their own life and interests." They maintain a "steady level of activity," and find any number of alternatives to justify their continued existence. In 1977, noted Cairns, one in nine Canadian workers worked for these two levels of government.

A consequence of this bureaucratization, adds Cairns, is not only that both politicians and the public become forces which "public servants must manage and manipulate," but that society as a whole becomes politicized and daily life invaded by government. Society is ever more under governments' "control and guidance," as they become the initiators of policy. Citizens are placed on the defensive, far too often forced to challenge government policies, whether in education, economics, welfare, health care, or even morality (for example, abortion). Citizens are not "the government," nor do they live in a true democracy, as social studies and political science courses try to convince students, but, as Jacek Kuron and Karol Modzelewski have pointed out (chapter 1), are increasingly its adversaries, trotted out occasionally for elections, and then put back on the shelf. We ought not be surprised. As Grant argued thirty years ago, only those whose interests are well-connected to this political and bureaucratic empire, namely, the corporate and media elites who really run this country, have any hope of serious influence over the decisions which shape the country's future.

Neo-liberal (and the general public's) criticism of the size and power of government, therefore, has much validity. Neo-liberal response to current political difficulties, however, goes beyond a desire to reduce government size, aiming, instead, to eliminate many of the services for which governments ought to be responsible, especially assistance for the poor who often lack the means for basic essentials such as food, shelter, clothing and medical care. Simply because governments are inefficient and bureaucratic, they ought not be abolished. Neo-liberal zeal to emasculate government will erode civil society and the public good, and may even lead to the disappearance of the state. As historian Christopher Lasch has noted, the neo-liberal world is a "tourist's" world, with commitments not to states, governments, or civic communities, but to international finance and globalization. Not only do neo-liberals want governments to cut services, they want them to cut the taxes which pay for these services. The wealthiest of the neo-liberals can well afford this attitude, as they jet-set from one walled environment to another, hire their own security services, pay for their own medical care, join private clubs, etc. Only the "freeloading" poor really need the state.

This neo-liberal attack on government seriously impairs peoples' ability to feel attached to their communities, their regions, and their country. In an article on homelessness in Canada, John Dalla Costa notes that current globalization pressures and processes are "rearranging Canadian social priorities" and "stress[ing] and fray[ing] what it means to be Canadian. Without a place to belong and grow, our youngest people are by default rendered rootless." But globalization by itself is not responsible for destroying Canadians' sense of home. It needed, he points out, the complicity of Canada's political leaders:

> After a decade of pursuing mostly economic agendas, federal and provincial policies have actually only undermined our roots and our sense of home. The ham-handed closing of hospitals, reorganization of schools and even the imposed amalgamation of cities are destabilizing and hurtful because they ignore the fact that, in their own way, each of these initiatives represents an emotional but nevertheless very real violation of home. At a time when the global economy is pulling us apart, our social institutions are proving largely ineffectual in keeping us together. We cannot generate much confidence for the future without the security and sense of social cohesion of roots.

Just as communities and regions pay the price when individuals suffer, so too is Canada undermined when its governments create policies and pass legislation weakening its regions.

Governments ought to exist and function for the well-being of *all* citizens: to ensure justice; to oversee the welfare of the commonwealth by safeguarding the well-being of the natural and man-made environments, whether by regulation or by providing infrastructure; and to regulate economic matters such as currency, banking, and taxes. In short, the proper task of governments is to maintain a healthy public arena, a place where matters of common concern can be fairly, openly, and freely dealt with, without fear, by all citizens. If government structures and legislative frameworks are presently failing to do what they should, they should not be dismantled as the neo-liberals suggest, but reformed.

It is not within the scope of this analysis to create and set out a blueprint for new governmental structures and arrangements at the federal and provincial levels. It is useful to note, however, that there is a growing body of literature suggesting frameworks for structural reforms — geo-economic regions, biodiversity zones, city-state regions, and so forth — which may cut across current provincial and even nation-state boundaries, and in which larger national and international organizations play crucial but varying advisory, supervisory, and regulatory roles.

Any such reforms must focus both on protecting the natural environment and on promoting the better functioning of civic communities and regions. Throughout Canada, the provincial governments, whatever their long-term future, will have to play a key role in this process because they control and administer about 90% of the country's crown land (93% in British Columbia). They are the ultimate authority and power over how most of Canada's land and resources are used. In British Columbia, for example, when the public blames the largely foreign-owned and financed resource (primarily forest and mining) industries for practices which diminish the province's natural environment and disrupt employment patterns, they ought also to be pointing their fingers at present and past provincial governments which both granted these companies the right to engage in these activities and sanctioned/subsidized the means by which they did so. Typically provincial governments have justified their roles and support for resource extraction industries by arguing that these activities created jobs and provided the basis for healthy regional and provincial economies. But as the resource industries automate, leave the natural environment desolate, lay off workers, and suck profits away from the workers and communities in which these industries operate and where the workers live, it is obvious that British Columbians must rethink how their crown land is used. As William Rees has noted, citizens become alienated from their immediate environment when "absentee landlords" control their resources and capital. He would agree with Mumford and Schumacher that people feel connected to their regions and communities when they have control over their resources, which, because they belong to all citizens, should not be set aside or exploited for the profit of a few. Corporate entities which do not treat local workers with respect, which deplete local resources, and whose success relies on non-renewable resource and transportation systems should be told to "take a hike."[3]

But granting control to people who actually live in the country's regions and establishing principles and practices for sustainability will be possible only through legislative initiatives by regional, provincial, and federal jurisdictions. There should be an end to tax breaks and subsidies for logging roads and highways, large-scale energy projects, agribusiness, and any use of non-renewable energy. They should be replaced with government support, tax breaks, and/or protectionist measures for public transit, small-scale, non-polluting energy projects, small-scale, bio-diverse, organic agriculture, and all activities which are virtually non-polluting and actively recycle, repair, reuse, and/or recondition. Large corporate chains should be prevented from setting up, and local businesses, supplied as much as possible with products from local resource and food bases, should be the rule rather than the exception. Big centralized health should, in most cases, be replaced by smaller clinics. Even government structures should be reformed to change the current imbalance in taxation, in which the largest share of tax dollars leaves communities for Ottawa, while the smallest amount is collected by local governments for local purposes. John Maynard Keynes articulated a useful principle in this regard: ideas, knowledge, and tourism are legitimately international, he said, but goods should be "homespun." This contrasts sharply with the current system of international trade, which is energy-wasteful, discourages local self-sufficiency, and exploits poorer parts of the globe where, under the control of the powerful trans-national corporations, food is grown, resources exploited, and cheaply priced goods manufactured for the wealthier peoples of the world.

In a country like Canada, thinking regionally and rethinking the roles of its cities will mean a radical re-orientation of the divisions of power and responsibility, in which regions and their cities are encouraged to strive toward self-reliance and self-sufficiency rather than being "branch-plants" of a central economy which in turn is reliant on outside, global, economic forces. The federal government should be the major instrument through which regional self-reliance, equality, and fairness are encouraged. In short, Canada needs a renewed federalism in which the federal government plays the crucial role in guaranteeing a playing field on which all the regions can play fairly. There must be a devolution of those powers that belong to the regions, with country-wide standards to ensure that one of the currently unmet promises of liberalism — namely, the well-being of individual citizens — is protected. This kind of renewed federalism, with sustainable, healthy regions, will be essential to maintaining a country which is more than just a country in name.

184

In an idealistic moment, economist Robert Heilbroner dreamed of a

> ... society whose mode of cooperation is neither custom and tradition, nor centralized command, nor subservience to market pressures and incentives. Its integrating principle would be *participation* — the engagement of all citizens in the mutual determination of every phase of their economic lives through discussion and voting.

People would work together to determine necessary tasks, the nature and volume of goods and services to be produced, and what each person's share should be. It would be "a world in which widely shared decision-making by discussion and vote displaces decision-making by self-interest alone, or by persons privileged by wealth or position to make unilateral determinations."

He is likely correct when he concludes that there is little possibility that such a world will exist in the near future.

NOTES

1 It is noteworthy that Canadians pay the highest rates of tax to the governments furthest away — the federal government takes the most, followed by the provincial government. Local and municipal governments take the smallest amounts, yet run the services which most affect our everyday lives.

2 The book of Genesis (Bible) notes that after Cain, the eldest child of Adam and Eve, built the first city for refuge following the murder of his brother, Abel, his descendants created the first technology and culture (tools and musical instruments). In the fourth-century BCE city-state of Athens, the male citizens, freed by women and slaves from the drudgery of labour, gave the world science, democracy, drama, and philosophy.

3 Alternative approaches to crown land and tree farm licenses do exist. See, for example, Drushka and Konttinen, *Tracks in the Forest,* an analysis of forestry in Finland where 75% of the forests are privately owned.

CONCLUSION:
DOES CANADA MATTER?

> To many modern men, the assumptions of this age
> appear inevitable, as being the expression of the
> highest wisdom that the race has distilled. The
> assumptions appear so inevitable that to entertain
> the possibility of their falsity may seem the work of a
> madman.
>
> — George Grant, *Lament for a Nation*

> . . . the battle will be won once people's ideas — not
> merely their feelings, those are already changing
> — change to the extent that they recognize the
> outdated vision of technological progress that would
> make the entire world into one gigantic suburb,
> with endlessly sprawling shopping malls or airports.
> — John Lukacs, *The End of the Twentieth Century*
> *and the End of the Modern Age*

In his conclusion to *Lament for a Nation,* George Grant won-
dered whether it was even worthwhile for Canadians to resist
the seemingly inevitable flow of history, namely, the homogenizing of all unique cultures and identities by the forces of liberalism, and to fight for a sovereign Canada. He noted:

. . . the question as to whether it is good that Canada should disappear must be left unsettled. If the best social order is the universal and homogeneous state, then the disappearance of Canada can be understood as a step toward that order. If the universal and homogeneous state would be a tyranny, then the disappearance of even this indigenous culture can be seen as the removal of a minor barrier on the road to that tyranny.

If the universal and homogeneous future is indeed what Canadians desire, then little more will be required of them but to watch (and applaud if they feel so inclined) as their media, corporate and political elites, utilizing the "advances" of modern science and technology, guide them to an ever more glorious future of increasing lifespans and dazzling arrays of consumer toys and gadgets, a world in which, as Rick Salutin notes, individuals "don't make ethical or political choices" but "shopping choices," where "life comes down to acquiring money and going shopping with the proceeds."

To Canadians dreaming of such a future, questioning the "course of history" or philosophizing about abstractions such as "the modern project," "the greater good," "horizons of significance," or "Canadian sovereignty" must seem anachronistic, reactionary, frivolous, and even ridiculous. In fact, at present, there is not much constructive value in dissent anyway, because, like most creations of the modern age, it has been commodified and trivialized. Quoting an advertising executive, writer Tom Frank notes:

The great brands . . . have succeeded in conveying their vision by questioning certain conventions, whether it's Apple's humanist vision, which reverses the relationship between people and machines; Benetton's libertarian vision, which overthrows communications conventions; Microsoft's progressive vision, which topples bureaucratic barriers; or Virgin's anticonformist vision, which rebels against the powers that be. The Body Shop owns compassion, Nike spirituality, Pepsi and MTV youthful rebellion. . . . The world of business is the world, period. There is nothing outside of it; it's a closed universe.

The encouragement of dissent as a tool to sell products has rendered it harmless and insignificant.

But there is another good reason why challenging the modern project may appear to be a waste of time, hopelessly pessimistic and tiresome. As Grant pointed out, in addition to material gain and individual happiness, the liberal dream promises fulfilment of one of humanity's deepest longings, namely, the desire for complete *freedom,* whether it be for people to choose who they may want to be, what they may want to think, or what they may want to do (and how they may want to do it). What could be better than such open-ended choice? And what could be more regressive than opposing such a lofty ideal?

Yet despite its seductive allure, liberal freedom often disappoints. Too frequently, that which is supposed to provide freedom turns out to be a bondage at least as bad as that from which people are supposedly being liberated. The automobile, for example, undoubtedly one of the twentieth century's most powerful symbols of freedom, has offered individuals a sense of choice and power, and has made everyday life easier for many. But there have been serious down-sides. Not only has the number of automobiles multiplied from 50 million in 1950, to over 400 million in 1990 — a major reason why the speed of traffic in major cities such as London is now slower than in the horse and buggy days of one hundred years ago — but the 225 billion gallons of non-renewable oil consumed in 1990 (eight times the consumption level of 1950), the internal combustion engine's role in air pollution (80% of pollution in most major North American cities), and the huge loss of life and medical costs, underscore the fact that the current widespread and growing use of the automobile is a social and environmental disaster. The freedom for all which the automobile promises — and has in many instances provided — is now becoming a problem for all. Freedom which threatens life is ultimately not freedom at all. A fish "freed" from water is not free.

Proponents of the modern project have an easy answer for the problems caused by the illusory freedom promised by liberalism. They assert that negative impacts of technological innovations such as the automobile or the computer are less a product of the technologies themselves than of the way in which they are used. In other words, they say, modern technology is "value-free," and whether it liberates (enriches) or enslaves results from user choice and taste rather than from the technology's intrinsic values and costs. They fail to mention that embedded in any technology is the world-view of its creators, their perspective of life that enabled them to create the technology in the first place.

Besides ignoring the embedded value-systems of technologies, advocates of the view that modern technology is value-free also conveniently overlook that the freedom ascribed to modern technology, like all "freedoms," has a price, and the price for modern technology's freedom is particularly high. Ursula Franklin has argued that the natural environment must always be factored in as a "value" in any assessment of modern technology: ". . . we need to consider machines and devices [technology] as cohabitants of this earth within the limiting parameters applied to human populations." She points out, for example, that if people are concerned about population control, they must apply the same sustainable criteria (carrying capacity) to technology and its products as they do to people. The creation and continued existence of machines and technology is not possible without their being fuelled by the earth's resources; hence, the permanent availability of these resources becomes critical. For one of the major users of non-renewable energy and resources, she suggests a rather bold prescription: "birth control for cars and trucks" as part of an overall "machine population control." The natural environment cannot afford the destructive consequences of a "free market" which allows the limitless production of goods such as automobiles.

But the values implicit in modern technology are not confined to the relationships among people, technology, freedom, and the natural environment. They go to the very premises of the modern project, which, as Gale Stokes has pointed out,

> [is] the Enlightenment view that humans, through the proper use of reason, could grasp the laws of human relations, just as Newton had grasped the laws of motion. In contrast with the Christian belief that humans are inherently evil, cursed with original sin that cannot be erased by human agency, [thinkers such as] Rousseau argued that people are inherently innocent . . . but that the organization of society . . . had created a situation in which evil could flourish. God's gift to human-kind was not sin, the Enlightenment taught us, but reason, whose proper use could provide the understanding and tools to right the wrongs. . . .

This utopian world-view guides today's global, corporate agenda. Will it work, and will history finally reach its apogee, having produced equitable and rational societies where everyone will live in complete freedom, having been released by modern technology from the drudgery of toil and exploitation, and liberated from subservience to nature?

If the answer is yes, then, as Grant has suggested, Canadians should simply withdraw their criticism, fold their tents, let Canada and its regions fade away into the homogeneous future, and watch history unfold to its natural and inevitable destiny. But what if the answer is no? What if Czech President Vaclav Havel is correct when he suggests that with the fall of the Soviet-dominated Eastern Bloc, the modern era has come to a final crisis, "the point beyond which the abyss begins"? He has argued:

> What is needed is something different, something larger. Man's attitude to the world must be radically changed. We have to abandon the arrogant belief that the world is merely a puzzle to be solved, a machine with instructions for use waiting to be discovered, a body of information to be fed into a computer in the hope that, sooner or later, it will spit out a universal solution. . . .
>
> We must try harder to understand than to explain. The way forward is not in the mere construction of universal systemic solutions, to be applied to reality from the outside; it is also in seeking to get to the heart of reality through personal experience. Such an approach promotes an atmosphere of tolerant solidarity and unity in diversity based on mutual respect, genuine pluralism, and parallelism. In a word, human uniqueness, human action, and the human spirit must be rehabilitated.

If he is correct, then Canadians had better come to terms with the obvious and increasing costs of treating nature and people as "objects" for manipulation by mechanistic science and technology. Furthermore, if they wish to protect the places where they live and which they call home as well as to provide a decent future (or one at all) for their offspring, they will have little choice but to challenge the modern project's simplistic and naive assumption that nature is merely a neutral canvas upon which humanity employs instrumental reason, science, and technology for its own betterment. They must acknowledge that there are consequences to the belief that humanity can (and has the right to) reshape life without after-effects. E.F. Schumacher has pointed out that

> the system of nature, of which man is a part, tends to be self-balancing, self-adjusting, self-cleansing. . . . In the subtle system of nature, technology, and in particular the super-technology of the modern world, acts like a foreign body, and there are now numerous signs of rejection.

Much of the responsibility for many of the potential human-made catastrophes which people currently face — from dirty air to polluted water — can, thus, be laid at the feet of the modern project. Rather than allowing the unfolding of the technological future and trying to mitigate negative consequences, perhaps Canadians should abandon certain ways of doing things altogether.

In the context of rethinking everyday practices and values, Canadians must come to terms with a fundamental truth about humanity: *of all creatures on earth, only human beings can consciously and deliberately alter the conditions of life.* The Bible states that human beings have "dominion" over other creatures. This should not be interpreted as an imperative, as some theologians would have us believe, but rather as a useful description of humanity's relationship with other forms of life, one requiring, even demanding, responsible, ethical stewardship. This means living with "nature," not separating it out as an abstraction, especially if it stands in the way of economic and industrial efficiency or contradicts environmentalist ideology. Canadians must learn and then practise basic economics ("household management"), so that they can experience being "at home" — a precondition for identity, security, and enrichment — and live comfortably and sustainably in their regions, cities, and communities.

How can they begin doing so? Part of the answer lies in adopting some of the measures suggested in the previous chapter, steps such as organizing grassroots and community groups, engaging in "appropriate" planning supported by legislation from senior governments, reconstituting cities and regions toward sustainable entities, and rethinking the roles and practices of senior and lower level governments. But these steps will not be enough. They will have to be accompanied by a more fundamental change. To save their country from the homogenizing, globalizing, corporatist ideals of the modern project, Canadians will have to rethink their personal and collective commitment/bondage to the values and myths of the liberal dream and the modern project.

In undertaking such rethinking, Canadians will find that their country's past will be of little assistance to them. For one thing, as a nation state, Canada has a short history. It is a young and immature country; its territorial extent was achieved only in 1949, and its internal boundaries are still being reshaped as its residents come to terms with its original peoples and with continuing streams of newcomers. More importantly, however, since confederation in 1867, there have been no alternatives to the liberal path of development and nation-building.

The key to the future, thus, lies not in returning to a romanticized past, as many neo-liberals would have us believe. In

194

true humility, as Havel has suggested for modern people generally, Canadians must try to "understand" rather than to "explain." They need new myths, ones which de-objectify reality, no longer treating the humans, animals, and plants with whom they live as objects whose ultimate well-being is of little concern. The Native people in my area claim that at one time their ancestors believed that they shared the world with all other creatures, that they were part of a broader community of "being," where mutual co-existence and concern was integral to the health and well-being of all. Or, as Martin Buber has put it, for humanity's physical and spiritual well-being, people must change their relationships with each other and with other forms of life from "I-It" (subject to object) to "I-Thou" (subject to subject).

These values must become fundamental for the millions of Canadians for whom the survival of Canada matters. While many younger Canadians may increasingly be willing to leave their country for "greener" economic pastures, there are many more for whom being Canadian is integral to their sense of well-being, even identity, whether they are the original inhabitants whose sole roots are in Canada, sixth- or seventh-generation Canadians, or recent arrivals who, while still having attachments to "the old country," see Canada as their adopted home, the place to raise their children as "Canadians."

But there is much more at stake here than simple feelings of attachment or sentiment. First of all, the survival of Canada as a unique, sovereign country — an archipelago with viable, sustainable, and locally-strong islands — matters because it will show the world that Canadians did not fold their tents in the face of liberalism's seductive lure, that they did not retreat powerlessly before the forces of globalization, and that they disproved the claims of modern ideologues who insisted that the disappearance of nation states into global homogeneity was both historically inevitable and necessary. It will demonstrate that, for Canadians, language, religion, political choice, economic activity, and social relationships had intrinsic value, that diversity in these fundamental aspects of life was more than a mere "lifestyle choice."

Secondly, the existence of a sovereign Canada would send a message to the world that Canada's governments recognized that nation-states have both the *choice* and the *power* to shift their loyalty from the corporate, media, and political elites to everyday people, that governments everywhere have the *option* and the *freedom* to transfer their allegiance from special interest groups to the common good, and that governments can *choose* to measure "progress" not only by the prosperity of its privileged few, but also by the well-being of its poor, its sick, and its unemployed, as well as of its natural environment.

Finally, Canadian sovereignty would demonstrate that the country's governments shifted Canada's reliance from those instruments which liberalism needs to thrive, namely, centralized economic systems, global trade mechanisms, and outside experts, to encouragement and support for initiatives which favoured not only local and regional (sustainable) stewardship of land, air, water, and trees, but also the maintenance and enhancement of people's special, even sacred, places and communities (rare in suburban environments), with their unique smells, sounds, sights, and ways of being and doing, those spots where people have what Rene Levesque called the "unmistakeable surety [that] they can be themselves" because they are "at home."

In short, Canada's continued existence as a sovereign country will serve as a litmus test for whether or not peoples, communities, cultures, and states around the globe can muster the will, the strength, and the courage successfully to stand up to the seductive lure and homogenizing tendencies of the modern project and of its illusory promise of "freedom."

For that reason especially, Canada does indeed matter.

SELECT BIBLIOGRAPHY

Acheson, T.W. "The National Policy and the Industrialization of the Maritimes." *Acadiensis* 1, Spring, 1972.

Alexander, Christopher; Ishikawa, Sara; Silverstein, Murray; et al. *A Pattern Language.* New York: Oxford University Press, 1977.

Arendt, Hannah. *The Human Condition.* Chicago: University of Chicago Press, 1958.

_____. *The Origins of Totalitarianism.* New York: Harcourt, Brace Jovanovich, 1973.

Barlow, Maude and Campbell, Bruce. *Take Back the Nation.* Toronto: Key Porter, 1991.

Barrett, William. *The Illusion of Technique.* Anchor City, New York: Anchor Books, 1978.

Baskerville, Peter. A. *Beyond the Island: An Illustrated History of Victoria.* Burlington, Ontario: Windsor, 1986.

Berton, Pierre. *1967: The Last Good Year.* Toronto: Doubleday, 1997.

Bliss, Michael. *A Living Profit: Studies in the Social History of Canadian Business, 1883-1911.* Toronto: McClelland & Stewart, 1974.

Brown, Lester. *Building a Sustainable Society.* New York: W.W. Norton, 1981.

Buber, Martin. *I and Thou.* New York: Charles Scribner's Sons, 1970.

Bumsted, J. M. "Canada and American Culture in the 1950s." *Bulletin of Canadian Studies,* IV, April 1980.

Cairns, Alan C. "The Governments and Societies of Canadian Federalism," in Mandel, Eli and Taras, David, eds. *A Passion for Identity: An Introduction to Canadian Studies.* Toronto: Methuen, 1987.

Calthorpe, Peter and Van der Ryn, Sim. *Sustainable Communities*. San Francisco: Sierra Club Books, 1986.

Canada, Government. *Report of the Royal Commission on Dominion-Provincial Relations, Book 1, Canada 1867-1939*. Ottawa, 1940.

CBC Ideas. "The Earth is not an Ecosystem." November 30-December 15, 1992. Contains interviews with Gustavo Esteva, Smithu Kothari, and Raimon Panikkar.

Careless, J.M.S. "The Lowe Brothers, 1852-70: A Study in Business Relations on the North Pacific Coast." *BC Studies*, 2, Summer, 1969.

Cassidy, John. "The Next Thinker: The Return of Karl Marx." *The New Yorker*, October 20-27, 1997.

Christian, William. *George Grant: A Biography*. Toronto: University of Toronto, 1994.

Clarke, Tony. *Silent Coup: Confronting the Big Business Takeover of Canada*. Toronto: James Lorimer, 1997.

Clay, John. "People, Not States, Make a Nation." (reprinted from *Mother Jones*), *Utne Reader*, July/August, 1992.

Costa, John Dalla. "At Home and Homeless." *The Financial Post Magazine*, March, 1998.

Crean, Susan and Rioux, Marcel. *Two Nations*. Toronto: James Lorimer and Co., 1983.

Cullingworth, J. B. *Urban and Regional Planning in Canada*. New Brunswick, New Jersey: Transaction Books, 1987.

Davies, Richard O. *The Age of Asphalt: The Automobile, the Freeway, and the Condition of Metropolitan America*. Toronto: J. B. Lippincott, 1975.

de Tocqueville, Alexis. *Democracy in America vols. 1 and 2*. New York: Alfred A. Knopf, 1945.

Drushka, Ken and Konttinen, Hannu. *Tracks in the Forest*. Madiera Park, British Columbia: Harbour, 1997.

Durning, Alan Thein. *This Place on Earth: Home and the Practice of Permanence*. Sasquatch Books, 1996.

Ellul, Jacques. *The Meaning of the City*. Grand Rapids, Michigan: Wm. B. Eerdmans, 1970.

―――. *The Technological Society*. New York: Alfred Knopf, 1964.

Elshtain, Jean-Bethke. *Democracy on Trial*. Concord, Ontario: Anansi, 1993.

Finkel, Alvin. "The Origins of the Welfare State in Canada" in Bumsted, J.M., *Interpreting Canada's Past,* Vol. II. Toronto: Oxford University, 1986.

Forward, C.N. ed. *Residential and Neighbourhood Studies in Victoria.* Victoria: University of Victoria, 1973.

Frank, Thomas C. *Conglomerates and the Media.* New York: New Press, 1997.

Franklin, Ursula. *The Real World of Technology.* Ottawa: CBC, 1990

Fukuyama, Francis. *The End of History and the Last Man.* New York: Free Press, 1992.

Gertler, L.O. *Regional Planning in Canada: A Planner's Testament.* Montreal: Harvest House, 1972.

Gibson, James R. *The Lifeline of the Oregon Country: The Fraser-Columbia Brigade System, 1811-1847.* Vancouver: UBC Press, 1997.

Grant, George. *Lament for a Nation: The Defeat of Canadian Nationalism.* Toronto: McClelland & Stewart, 1965.

———. *Philosophy in the Mass Age.* Sackville, New Brunswick: Mount Allison University, 1974.

———. *Technology and Empire: Perspectives on North America.* Toronto: Anansi, 1969.

———. *Technology and Justice.* Toronto: Anansi, 1986.

———. *Time as History.* Toronto: CBC, 1969.

Gwyn, Richard. *Nationalism Without Walls: The Unbearable Lightness of Being Canadian.* Toronto: McClelland & Stewart, 1996.

Haar, Charles. ed. *The End of Innocence: A Suburban Reader.* Glenview, Illinois: Scott, Foresman and Co., 1972.

Harris, R. Cole. "Regionalism and the Canadian Archipelago" in L.D. McCann, ed., *Heartland and Hinterland: A Geography of Canada.* Scarborough, 1982.

Havel, Vaclav. *Summer Meditations.* Toronto: Vintage, 1993.

Heilbroner, Robert. *Twenty-first Century Capitalism.* Concord, Ontario: Anansi, 1992.

Hiss, Tony. *The Experience of Place.* New York: Alfred A. Knopf, 1991.

Hurtig, Mel. *The Betrayal of Canada.* Toronto: Stoddart, 1992.

Huston, Nancy. "A Bucking Nightmare." *Saturday Night,* June, 1997.

Innis, Harold. *The Bias of Communication*. Toronto: University of Toronto, Press, 1951.

_____. *Empire and Communications*. London: Oxford University Press, 1950.

_____. *The Fur Trade in Canada: An Introduction to Canadian Economic History*. New Haven: Yale University Press, 1930.

Jackson, Kenneth. "Race, Ethnicity and Real Estate Appraisal." *Journal of Urban History*, August, 1980.

Jacobs, Jane. *Cities and the Wealth of Nations*. New York: Random House, 1984.

Kaplan, Robert. D. *The Ends of the Earth: A Journey at the Dawn of the 21st Century*. New York: Random House, 1996.

Keynes, John M. *The General Theory of Employment, Interest & Money*. New York: Harcourt, Brace & World, 1936.

Kingwell, Mark. *Better Living: In Pursuit of Happiness from Plato to Prozac*. Toronto: Viking, 1998.

Kluckner, Michael. *Paving Paradise: Is British Columbia Losing its Heritage?* Vancouver: Whitecap Books, 1991.

Kroker, Arthur. *Technology and the Canadian Mind: Innis/McLuhan/Grant*. Montreal: New World Perspectives, 1984.

Kuhn, Thomas S. *The Structure of Scientific Revolutions*. Chicago: University of Chicago Press, 1970.

Kunstler, James Howard. *The Geography of Nowhere: The Rise and Decline of America's Man-Made Landscape*. New York: Touchstone, 1993.

Kuron, Jacek and Modzelewski, Karol. "Open Letter to the Party" in Stokes, Gale ed., *From Stalinism to Pluralism: A Documentary History of Eastern Europe Since 1945* (second edition). New York: Oxford University Press, 1966: 108-114.

Lasch, Christopher. *The Revolt of the Elites and the Betrayal of Democracy*. New York: W.W. Norton, 1995.

Levesque, Rene. "A Country that Must be Made" in *An Option for Quebec*. Toronto: McClelland & Stewart, 1968.

Logan, John R. and Molotch, Harvey L. *Urban Fortunes: The Political Economy of Space*. Berkeley and Los Angeles: University of California Press, 1987.

Loreto, Richard A. and Price, Trevor, eds. *Urban Policy Issues: Canadian Perspectives.* Toronto: McClelland & Stewart, 1990.

Lukacs, John. *The End of the Twentieth Century and the End of the Modern Age.* New York: Ticknor and Fields, 1993.

Lustiger-Thaler, Henri. *Political Arrangements: Power and the City.* Montreal: Black Rose Books, 1993.

McBride, Stephen and Shields, John. *Dismantling a Nation: Canada and the New World Order.* Halifax: Fernwood Publishing, 1993.

McDonald, Robert A.J. "Victoria, Vancouver, and the Economic Development of British Columbia, 1886-1914" in Artibise, Alan F. J. *Town and City: Aspects of Western Canadian Urban Development.* Regina: Canadian Plains Research Centre, 1981.

McQuaig, Linda. *Shooting the Hippo: Death by Deficit and other Canadian Myths.* Toronto: Viking, 1995.

_____. *The Quick and the Dead: Brian Mulroney, Big Business and the Seduction of Canada.* Toronto: Penguin, 1992.

_____. *The Cult of Impotence: Selling the Myth of Powerlessness in the Global Economy.* Toronto: Viking, 1998.

Mackie, Richard Somerset. *Trading Beyond the Mountains: The British Fur Trade on the Pacific, 1793-1843.* Vancouver: UBC Press, 1997.

Mandel, Eli and Taras, David, eds. *A Passion for Identity: An Introduction to Canadian Studies.* Toronto: Methuen, 1987.

Meadows, Donella H. et al. *The Limits to Growth: A Report for the Club of Rome's Project on the Predicament of Mankind.* New York: Universe Books, 1972.

Melody, William H., Salter, Liora R., and Heyer, Paul, eds. *Culture, Communications and Dependency: The Tradition of H.A. Innis.* Norwood, New Jersey: Ablex, 1981.

Morton, W.L. "Confederation, 1870-1896: The End of the Macdonaldian Constitution and the Return to Duality." *Journal of Canadian Studies,* 1, May, 1966.

Mumford, Lewis. *The City in History.* New York: Harcourt, Brace and World, 1961.

_____. *The Culture of Cities.* New York: Harcourt, Brace and Co., 1938.

_____. *Technics and Civilization.* New York: Harcourt, Brace and World, 1963.

Norberg-Hodge, Helena. "News From Next Door." *New Internationalist,* August, 1996.

Norrie, Kenneth and Owram, Douglas. *A History of the Canadian Economy.* Toronto: Harcourt Brace Jovanovich, Canada, 1991.

Polanyi, Michael and Prosch, Harry. *Meaning.* Chicago: University of Chicago Press, 1975.

Postman, Neil. *Technopoly: The Surrender of Culture to Technology.* New York: Alfred A. Knopf, 1992.

Ralston, Keith. "Patterns of Trade and Investment on the Pacific Coast, 1867-1892: The Case of British Columbia Salmon Canning." *BC Studies,* No. 1, Winter 1968-69.

Rees, William E. "Revisiting Carrying Capacity: Area-Based Indicators of Sustainability." Presented to the International Workshop of Evaluation Criteria for a Sustainable Economy, 6-7 April, 1994.

Robin, Martin. *The Company Province: 2 vols.* Toronto: McClelland & Stewart, 1972.

Roseland, Mark. *Toward Sustainable Communities.* Ottawa: National Round Table on the Environment and the Economy, 1992.

Roszak, Theodore. *Where the Wasteland Ends: Politics and Transcendence in Postindustrial Society.* Garden City, New York: Anchor Books, 1973.

Sachs, Wolfgang. "Development, A Guide to the Ruins." *New Internationalist,* June, 1992.

Saige, Franklin. "Mega-buys: All Roads on the Info Superhighway Lead to More Consumption." *Plain,* Spring 1994.

Salutin, Rick. "A Plea for Canada." *Maclean's,* 1 July, 1995.

Saul, John Ralston. *Reflections of a Siamese Twin: Canada at the End of the Twentieth Century.* Toronto: Viking, 1997.

_____. *The Unconscious Civilization.* Concord, Ontario: Anansi, 1995.

Schumacher, E.F. *Small is Beautiful: A Study of Economics as if People Really Mattered.* London: Penguin, 1989.

Shafer, Thomas W. *Urban Growth and Economics.* Reston, Virginia: Reston Publishing Co., 1977.

Sinclair, Peter R. "Class Structure and Populist Protest: The Case of Western Canada." *Canadian Journal of Sociology,* I, 1975.

Spretnak, Charlene. "Resurgence of the Real." *Utne Reader,* July-August, 1997

Stokes, Gale, ed,. *From Stalinism to Pluralism: A Documentary History of Eastern Europe Since 1945* (second edition). New York: Oxford University Press, 1966.

Taylor, Charles. *The Malaise of Modernity.* Concord, Ontario: Anansi, 1991.

Wackernagel, Mathis and Rees, William. *Our Ecological Footprint: Reducing Human Impact on the Earth.* Gabriola Island, British Columbia: New Society Publishers, 1986.

Walljasper, Jay. "Who Paints the future?" *Utne Reader,* No. 85 Jan-Feb, 1998.

INDEX

ABOUT THE AUTHOR

Clarence Bolt is an instructor of modern history at Camosun College in Victoria, BC. A native of British Columbia, he has extensive experience in local politics, having served on the executives of various citizens groups, on government committees and boards, and on the municipal council of his community. He served a brief stint as a researcher writer for the Carrier Sekani Tribal Council, and is the author of *Small Shoes for Feet Too Large: Thomas Crosby and the Tsimshian* (1992). He lives with his wife in Central Saanich, a small rural/suburban community 10 kilometers outside of Victoria.